Harold Pinter

Plays : Two

The Caretaker, The Dwarfs,
The Collection, The Lover, Night School,
Trouble in the Works, The Black and White, Request Stop,
Last to Go, Special Offer

Harold Pinter is the most original writer to have emerged from the 'new wave' of dramatists who gave fresh life to the British theatre in the late fifties and early sixties. He is now firmly established as 'our best living playwright' (*The Times*).

This book is Volume Two of the Collected Plays of Harold Pinter. It contains his best-known play, *The Caretaker*, which was his first big success (in 1960), plus the four shorter plays which followed. Sketching in the background to these plays is a 1961 interview with Pinter, which introduces the volume. Also included are five revue sketches written during the same period.

Harold Pinter was born in London in 1930. He wrote his first plays, The Room, The Birthday Party *and* The Dumb Waiter, *in 1957 and achieved his first great success with* The Caretaker *in 1960. Since then he has written four more full-length plays,* The Homecoming *(1964),* Old Times *(1970),* No Man's Land *(1974) and* Betrayal *(1978), as well as a number of shorter plays for the stage, radio and television. For the cinema, his screenplays include* The Servant, Accident, The Go-Between, À la Recherche du Temps perdu *(published as* The Proust Screenplay*),* The Last Tycoon *and* The French Lieutenant's Woman. The Hothouse *was first performed in 1980. An early version of his triple-bill,* Other Places, *was seen at the National Theatre in 1982; now consisting of the three Plays* Victoria Station, A Kind of Alaska *and* One For The Road, *it played in the West End in 1985.*

by the same author

in Methuen's Modern Plays

BETRAYAL
THE BIRTHDAY PARTY
THE CARETAKER
THE COLLECTION *and* THE LOVER
THE HOMECOMING
THE HOTHOUSE
LANDSCAPE *and* SILENCE
NO MAN'S LAND
OLD TIMES
OTHER PLACES
(*A Kind of Alaska, Victoria Station, Family Voices*)
ONE FOR THE ROAD
THE ROOM *and* THE DUMB WAITER
A SLIGHT ACHE *and other plays*
TEA PARTY *and other plays*

in the World Dramatists series

PLAYS : ONE
(The Birthday Party, The Room, The Dumb Waiter, A Slight
Ache, The Hothouse, A Night Out)

PLAYS : THREE
(The Homecoming, Tea Party, The Basement, Landscape,
Silence)

PLAYS : FOUR
(Old Times, No Man's Land, Betrayal, Monologue, Family
Voices)

also available

THE PROUST SCREENPLAY – *À la Recherche du Temps Perdu*
POEMS AND PROSE 1949–1977
FIVE SCREENPLAYS
(The Servant, The Pumpkin Eater, The Quiller Memorandum,
Accident, The Go-Between)
THE FRENCH LIEUTENANT'S WOMAN
and other screenplays

HAROLD PINTER
Plays : Two

The Caretaker
The Dwarfs
The Collection
The Lover
Night School
Trouble in the Works
The Black and White
Request Stop
Last to Go
Special Offer

With an introduction : 'Writing for Myself'

Methuen Drama

Methuen's World Dramatists

This collection first published in 1977 by Eyre Methuen Ltd
Reprinted 1979 with revised version of *Night School*
Reprinted 1981
Reprinted 1983, 1986 by Methuen London Ltd
Reprinted in 1988 by Methuen Drama, Michelin House,
81 Fulham Road, London SW3 6RB

The Caretaker first published by Methuen & Co. in 1960, revised in 1962
*The Dwarfs, Trouble in the Works, The Black and White, Request Stop,
Last to Go* first published by Methuen & Co. in 1961, corrected in 1968
The Collection, The Lover first published by Methuen & Co. in 1963,
second edition in 1964
Night School (television version) first published in 1979 reprint of this
collection
Special Offer first published in *Harold Pinter* by Arnold P. Hinchcliffe,
Twayne, New York, 1967
'Writing for Myself' first appeared in *The Twentieth Century*, February,
1961

Set, printed and bound in Great Britain by
Cox & Wyman Ltd, Reading

ISBN 0 413 37300 2

Contents

Chronology   *page* 7
Introduction: Writing for Myself   9
THE CARETAKER   13
THE DWARFS   89
THE COLLECTION   119
THE LOVER   159
NIGHT SCHOOL   197
REVUE SKETCHES   239
   Trouble in the Works   241
   The Black and White   244
   Request Stop   247
   Last to Go   249
   Special Offer   253

Harold Pinter : A Chronology

Year of writing

First performance

1954–5	The Black and White	(short story)
1955	The Examination	(short story)
1957	The Room	15 May 1957
1957	The Birthday Party	28 April 1958
1957	The Dumb Waiter	21 January 1960
1958	The Hothouse	25 April 1980
1958	A Slight Ache	29 July 1959
1959	Revue sketches—	
	Trouble in the Works; The Black and White	15 July 1959
	Request Stop; Last to Go; Special Offer	23 September 1959
	That's Your Trouble; That's All; Applicant; Interview; Dialogue for Three	February–March 1964
1959	A Night Out	1 March 1960
1959	The Caretaker	27 April 1960
1960	Night School	21 July 1960
1960	The Dwarfs	2 December 1960
1961	The Collection	11 May 1961
1962	The Lover	28 March 1963
1963	Tea Party	(short story)
1964	Tea Party	25 March 1965
1964	The Homecoming	3 June 1965
1966	The Basement	28 February 1967
1967	Landscape	25 April 1968
1968	Silence	2 July 1969
1969	Night	9 April 1969
1970	Old Times	1 June 1971
1972	Monologue	10 April 1973
1974	No Man's Land	23 April 1975
1978	Betrayal	15 November 1978
1980	Family Voices	22 January 1981
1982	Victoria Station	performed with
	A Kind of Alaska	Family Voices as a trilogy entitled Other Places in 1982
1984	One for the Road	13 March 1984

Introduction

Writing for Myself

Based on a conversation with Richard Findlater published in The Twentieth Century, *February 1961.*

The first time I went to a theatre, as far as I remember, was to see Donald Wolfit in Shakespeare. I saw his Lear six times, and later acted with him in it, as one of the king's knights. I saw very few plays, in fact, before I was twenty. Then I acted in too many. I did eighteen months in Ireland with Anew McMaster, playing one-night stands in fit-ups, and I've worked all over the place in reps – Huddersfield, Torquay, Bournemouth, Whitby, Colchester, Birmingham, Chesterfield, Worthing, Palmers Green and Richmond. I was an actor for about nine years (under the name of David Baron) and I would like to do more. I played Goldberg in *The Birthday Party* at Cheltenham recently, and enjoyed it very much. I'd like to play that part again. Yes, my experience as an actor has influenced my plays – it must have – though it's impossible for me to put my finger on it exactly. I think I certainly developed some feeling for construction which, believe it or not, is important to me, and for speakable dialogue. I had a pretty good notion in my earlier plays of what would shut an audience up; not so much what would make them laugh; that I had no ideas about. Whenever I write for the stage I merely see the stage I've been used to. I have worked for theatre in the round and enjoyed it, but it doesn't move me to write plays with that method in mind. I always think of the normal picture-frame stage which I used as an actor.

All the time I was acting I was writing. Not plays. Hundreds of poems – about a dozen are worth republishing – and short prose pieces. A lot of these were in dialogue, and one was a monologue which I later turned into a revue sketch. I also wrote a novel. It was autobiographical, to a certain extent, based on part of my youth in Hackney. I wasn't the central

character, though I appeared in it in disguise. The trouble
about the novel was that it was stretched out over too long a
period, and it incorporated too many styles, so that it became
rather a hotch-potch. But I've employed certain strains in the
book which I thought were worth exploring in my radio play
The Dwarfs. That was the title of the novel.

I didn't start writing plays until 1957. I went into a room
one day and saw a couple of people in it. This stuck with me for
some time afterwards, and I felt that the only way I could give
it expression and get it off my mind was dramatically. I started
off with this picture of the two people and let them carry on
from there. It wasn't a deliberate switch from one kind of
writing to another. It was quite a natural movement. A friend
of mine, Henry Woolf, produced the result – *The Room* – at
Bristol University, and a few months later in January 1958 it
was included – in a different production – in the festival of
university drama. Michael Codron heard about this play and
wrote to me at once to ask if I had a full-length play. I had
just finished *The Birthday Party* . . . .

I start off with people, who come into a particular situation.
I certainly don't write from any kind of abstract idea. And I
wouldn't know a symbol if I saw one. I don't see that there's
anything very strange about *The Caretaker*, for instance, and I
can't quite understand why so many people regard it in the
way they do. It seems to me a very straightforward and simple
play. The germ of my plays? I'll be as accurate as I can about
that. I went into a room and saw one person standing up and
one person sitting down, and a few weeks later I wrote *The
Room*. I went into another room and saw two people sitting
down, and a few years later I wrote *The Birthday Party*. I looked
through a door into a third room, and saw two people standing
up and I wrote *The Caretaker*.

I don't write with any audience in mind. I just write. I take
a chance on the audience. That's what I did originally, and I
think it's worked – in the sense that I find there *is* an audience.

If you've got something you want to say to the world, then you'd be worried that only a few thousand people might see your play. Therefore you'd do something else. You'd become a religious teacher, or a politician perhaps. But if you don't want to give some particular message to the world, explicitly and directly, you just carry on writing, and you're quite content. I was always surprised that anyone initially came in to see my plays at all, because writing them was a very personal thing. I did it – and still do it – for my own benefit; and it's pure accident if anyone else happens to participate. Firstly and finally, and all along the line, you write because there's something you *want* to write, *have* to write. For yourself.

I'm convinced that what happens in my plays could happen anywhere, at any time, in any place, although the events may seem unfamiliar at first glance. If you press me for a definition, I'd say that what goes on in my plays is realistic, but what I'm doing is not realism.

Writing for television? I don't make any distinction between kinds of writing, but when I write for the stage I always keep a continuity of action. Television lends itself to quick cutting from scene to scene, and nowadays I see it more and more in terms of pictures. When I think of someone knocking at a door, I see the door opening in close-up and a long shot of someone going up the stairs. Of course the words go with the pictures, but on television, ultimately, the words are of less importance than they are on the stage. A play I wrote called *A Night Out* did, I think, successfully integrate the picture and the words, although that may be because I wrote it first for radio. Sixteen million people saw that on television. That's very difficult to grasp. You can't even think about it. And when you write for television, you don't think about it. I don't find television confining or restrictive, and it isn't limited to realism, necessarily. Its possibilities go well beyond that. I have one or two ideas in my mind at the moment which wouldn't be very realistic and which might be quite effective on television.

I like writing for sound radio, because of the freedom. When I wrote *The Dwarfs* a few months ago, I was able to experiment in form – a mobile, flexible structure, more flexible and mobile than in any other medium. And from the point of view of content I was able to go the whole hog and enjoy myself by exploring to a degree which wouldn't be acceptable in any other medium. I'm sure the result may have been completely incomprehensible to the audience, but it isn't as far as I'm concerned, and it was extremely valuable to me.

No, I'm not committed as a writer, in the usual sense of the term, either religiously or politically. And I'm not conscious of any particular social function. I write because I want to write. I don't see any placards on myself, and I don't carry any banners. Ultimately I distrust definitive labels. As far as the state of the theatre is concerned, I'm as conscious as anyone else of the flaws of procedure, of taste, of the general set-up in management, and I think things will go on more or less as they are for some considerable time. But it seems to me that there has been a certain development in one channel or another in the past three years. *The Caretaker* wouldn't have been put on, and certainly wouldn't have run, before 1957. The old categories of comedy and tragedy and farce are irrelevant, and the fact that managers seem to have realized that is one favourable change. But writing for the stage is the most difficult thing of all, whatever the system. I find it more difficult the more I think about it.

The Caretaker

This play was first presented by the Arts Theatre Club in association with Michael Codron and David Hall at the Arts Theatre, London, WC2, on 27th April, 1960.

On 30th May, 1960, the play was presented by Michael Codron and David Hall at the Duchess Theatre, London, with the following cast:

MICK, *a man in his late twenties*	Alan Bates
ASTON, *a man in his early thirties*	Peter Woodthorpe
DAVIES, *an old man*	Donald Pleasence

The play was directed by Donald McWhinnie

On 2nd March, 1972, a revival of the play directed by Christopher Morahan was presented at the Mermaid Theatre, London, with the following cast:

MICK	John Hurt
ASTON	Jeremy Kemp
DAVIES	Leonard Rossiter

The action of the play takes place in a house in west London

ACT I A night in winter
ACT II A few seconds later
ACT III A fortnight later

A room. A window in the back wall, the bottom half covered by a sack. An iron bed along the left wall. Above it a small cupboard, paint buckets, boxes containing nuts, screws, etc. More boxes, vases, by the side of the bed. A door, up right. To the right of the window, a mound: a kitchen sink, a step-ladder, a coal bucket, a lawn-mower, a shopping trolley, boxes, sideboard drawers. Under this mound an iron bed. In front of it a gas stove. On the gas stove a statue of Buddha. Down right, a fireplace. Around it a couple of suitcases, a rolled carpet, a blow-lamp, a wooden chair on its side, boxes, a number of ornaments, a clothes horse, a few short planks of wood, a small electric fire and a very old electric toaster. Below this a pile of old newspapers. Under ASTON'S *bed by the left wall, is an electrolux, which is not seen till used. A bucket hangs from the ceiling.*

Act One

MICK *is alone in the room, sitting on the bed. He wears a leather jacket.*

Silence.

He slowly looks about the room looking at each object in turn. He looks up at the ceiling, and stares at the bucket. Ceasing, he sits quite still, expressionless, looking out front.

Silence for thirty seconds.

A door bangs. Muffled voices are heard.

MICK *turns his head. He stands, moves silently to the door, goes out, and closes the door quietly.*

Silence.

Voices are heard again. They draw nearer, and stop. The door opens. ASTON *and* DAVIES *enter,* ASTON *first,* DAVIES *following, shambling, breathing heavily.*

ASTON *wears an old tweed overcoat, and under it a thin shabby dark-blue pinstripe suit, single-breasted, with a pullover and faded shirt and tie.* DAVIES *wears a worn brown overcoat, shapeless trousers, a waistcoat, vest, no shirt, and sandals.* ASTON *puts the key in his pocket and closes the door.* DAVIES *looks about the room.*

ASTON. Sit down.

DAVIES. Thanks. (*Looking about.*) Uuh. . . .

ASTON. Just a minute.

> ASTON *looks around for a chair, sees one lying on its side by the rolled carpet at the fireplace, and starts to get it out.*

DAVIES. Sit down? Huh . . . I haven't had a good sit down . . . I haven't had a proper sit down . . . well, I couldn't tell you. . . .

ASTON (*placing the chair*). Here you are.

DAVIES. Ten minutes off for a tea-break in the middle of the night in that place and I couldn't find a seat, not one. All them Greeks had it, Poles, Greeks, Blacks, the lot of them, all them aliens had it. And they had me working there . . . they had me working. . . .

> ASTON *sits on the bed, takes out a tobacco tin and papers, and begins to roll himself a cigarette.* DAVIES *watches him.*

All them Blacks had it, Blacks, Greeks, Poles, the lot of them, that's what, doing me out of a seat, treating me like dirt. When he come at me tonight I told him.

> *Pause.*

ASTON. Take a seat.

DAVIES. Yes, but what I got to do first, you see, what I got to do, I got to loosen myself up, you see what I mean? I could have got done in down there.

> DAVIES *exclaims loudly, punches downward with closed fist, turns his back to* ASTON *and stares at the wall.*
> *Pause.* ASTON *lights a cigarette.*

ASTON. You want to roll yourself one of these?

DAVIES (*turning*). What? No, no, I never smoke a cigarette. (*Pause. He comes forward.*) I'll tell you what, though. I'll have a bit of that tobacco there for my pipe, if you like.

ASTON (*handing him the tin*). Yes. Go on. Take some out of that.

DAVIES. That's kind of you, mister. Just enough to fill my pipe, that's all. (*He takes a pipe from his pocket and fills it.*) I had a tin, only . . . only a while ago. But it was knocked off. It was knocked off on the Great West Road. (*He holds out the tin*). Where shall I put it?

ASTON. I'll take it.

DAVIES (*handing the tin*). When he come at me tonight I told him. Didn't I? You heard me tell him, didn't you?

ASTON. I saw him have a go at you.

DAVIES. Go at me? You wouldn't grumble. The filthy skate, an old man like me, I've had dinner with the best.

Pause.

ASTON. Yes, I saw him have a go at you.

DAVIES. All them toe-rags, mate, got the manners of pigs. I might have been on the road a few years but you can take it from me I'm clean. I keep myself up. That's why I left my wife. Fortnight after I married her, no, not so much as that, no more than a week, I took the lid off a saucepan, you know what was in it? A pile of her underclothing, unwashed. The pan for vegetables, it was. The vegetable pan. That's when I left her and I haven't seen her since.

DAVIES *turns, shambles across the room, comes face to face with a statue of Buddha standing on the gas stove, looks at it and turns.*

I've eaten my dinner off the best of plates. But I'm not young any more. I remember the days I was as handy as any of them. They didn't take any liberties with me. But I haven't been so well lately. I've had a few attacks.

Pause.

(*Coming closer.*) Did you see what happened with that one?

ASTON. I only got the end of it.

DAVIES. Comes up to me, parks a bucket of rubbish at me tells me to take it out the back. It's not my job to take out the bucket! They got a boy there for taking out the bucket. I wasn't engaged to take out buckets! My job's cleaning the floor, clearing up the tables, doing a bit of washing-up, nothing to do with taking out buckets!

ASTON. Uh.

He crosses down right, to get the electric toaster.

DAVIES (*following*). Yes, well say I had! Even if I had! Even if I was supposed to take out the bucket, who was this git to

come up and give me orders? We got the same standing.
He's not my boss. He's nothing superior to me.

ASTON. What was he, a Greek?

DAVIES. Not him, he was a Scotch. He was a Scotchman.
(ASTON *goes back to his bed with the toaster and starts to
unscrew the plug.* DAVIES *follows him*). You got an eye of him,
did you?

ASTON. Yes.

DAVIES. I told him what to do with his bucket. Didn't I? You
heard. Look here, I said, I'm an old man, I said, where I was
brought up we had some idea how to talk to old people with
the proper respect, we was brought up with the right ideas,
if I had a few years off me I'd . . . I'd break you in half.
That was after the guvnor give me the bullet. Making too
much commotion, he says. Commotion, me! Look here, I
said to him, I got my rights. I told him that. I might have
been on the road but nobody's got more rights than I have.
Let's have a bit of fair play, I said. Anyway, he give me the
bullet. (*He sits in the chair*). That's the sort of place.
    Pause.
If you hadn't come out and stopped that Scotch git I'd be
inside the hospital now. I'd have cracked my head on that
pavement if he'd have landed. I'll get him. One night I'll get
him. When I find myself around that direction.
    ASTON *crosses to the plug box to get another plug.*
I wouldn't mind so much but I left all my belongings in that
place, in the back room there. All of them, the lot there was,
you see, in this bag. Every lousy blasted bit of all my bleeding belongings I left down there now. In the rush of it. I bet
he's having a poke around in it now this very moment.

ASTON. I'll pop down sometime and pick them up for you.

    ASTON *goes back to his bed and starts to fix the plug on the
    toaster.*

DAVIES. Anyway, I'm obliged to you, letting me . . . letting me have a bit of a rest, like . . . for a few minutes. (*He looks about.*) This your room?

ASTON. Yes.

DAVIES. You got a good bit of stuff here.

ASTON. Yes.

DAVIES. Must be worth a few bob, this . . . put it all together.

Pause.

There's enough of it.

ASTON. There's a good bit of it, all right.

DAVIES. You sleep here, do you?

ASTON. Yes.

DAVIES. What, in that?

ASTON. Yes.

DAVIES. Yes, well, you'd be well out of the draught there.

ASTON. You don't get much wind.

DAVIES. You'd be well out of it. It's different when you're kipping out.

ASTON. Would be.

DAVIES. Nothing but wind then.

Pause.

ASTON. Yes, when the wind gets up it. . . .

Pause.

DAVIES. Yes. . . .

ASTON. Mmnn. . . .

Pause.

DAVIES. Gets very draughty.

ASTON. Ah.

DAVIES. I'm very sensitive to it.

ASTON. Are you?

DAVIES. Always have been.

Pause.

You got any more rooms then, have you?

ASTON. Where?

DAVIES. I mean, along the landing here . . . up the landing there.

ASTON. They're out of commission.

DAVIES. Get away.

ASTON. They need a lot of doing to.

Slight pause.

DAVIES. What about downstairs?

ASTON. That's closed up. Needs seeing to. . . . The floors. . . .

Pause.

DAVIES. I was lucky you come into that caff. I might have been done by that Scotch git. I been left for dead more than once.

Pause.

I noticed that there was someone was living in the house next door.

ASTON. What?

DAVIES. (*gesturing*). I noticed. . . .

ASTON. Yes. There's people living all along the road.

DAVIES. Yes, I noticed the curtains pulled down there next door as we came along.

ASTON. They're neighbours.

Pause.

DAVIES. This your house then, is it?

Pause.

ASTON. I'm in charge.

DAVIES. You the landlord, are you?

He puts a pipe in his mouth and puffs without lighting it.

Yes, I noticed them heavy curtains pulled across next door

as we came along. I noticed them heavy big curtains right across the window down there. I thought there must be someone living there.

ASTON. Family of Indians live there.

DAVIES. Blacks?

ASTON. I don't see much of them.

DAVIES. Blacks, eh? (DAVIES *stands and moves about*.) Well you've got some knick-knacks here all right, I'll say that. I don't like a bare room. (ASTON *joins* DAVIES *upstage centre*). I'll tell you what, mate, you haven't got a spare pair of shoes?

ASTON. Shoes?

ASTON *moves downstage right*.

DAVIES. Them bastards at the monastery let me down again.

ASTON. (*going to his bed*.) Where?

DAVIES. Down in Luton. Monastery down at Luton. . . . I got a mate at Shepherd's Bush, you see. . . .

ASTON (*looking under his bed*). I might have a pair.

DAVIES. I got this mate at Shepherd's Bush. In the convenience. Well, he was in the convenience. Run about the best convenience they had. (*He watches* ASTON.) Run about the best one. Always slipped me a bit of soap, any time I went in there. Very good soap. They have to have the best soap. I was never without a piece of soap, whenever I happened to be knocking about the Shepherd's Bush area.

ASTON (*emerging from under the bed with shoes*). Pair of brown.

DAVIES. He's gone now. Went. He was the one who put me on to this monastery. Just the other side of Luton. He'd heard they give away shoes.

ASTON. You've got to have a good pair of shoes.

DAVIES. Shoes? It's life and death to me. I had to go all the way to Luton in these.

ASTON. What happened when you got there, then?

Pause.

DAVIES. I used to know a bootmaker in Acton. He was a good mate to me.

Pause.

You know what that bastard monk said to me?

Pause.

How many more Blacks you got around here then?

ASTON. What?

DAVIES. You got any more Blacks around here?

ASTON (*holding out the shoes*). See if these are any good.

DAVIES. You know what that bastard monk said to me? (*He looks over to the shoes.*) I think those'd be a bit small.

ASTON. Would they?

DAVIES. No, don't look the right size.

ASTON. Not bad trim.

DAVIES. Can't wear shoes that don't fit. Nothing worse. I said to this monk, here, I said, look here, mister, he opened the door, big door, he opened it, look here, mister, I said, I come all the way down here, look, I said, I showed him these, I said, you haven't got a pair of shoes, have you, a pair of shoes, I said, enough to keep me on my way. Look at these, they're nearly out, I said, they're no good to me. I heard you got a stock of shoes here. Piss off, he said to me. Now look here, I said, I'm an old man, you can't talk to me like that, I don't care who you are. If you don't piss off, he says, I'll kick you all the way to the gate. Now look here, I said, now wait a minute, all I'm asking for is a pair of shoes, you don't want to start taking liberties with me, it's taken me three days to get here, I said to him, three days without a bite, I'm worth a bite to eat, en I? Get out round the corner to the kitchen, he says, get out round the corner, and when you've had your meal, piss off out of it. I went round to this kitchen, see? Meal they give me! A bird, I tell you, a little

bird, a little tiny bird, he could have ate it in under two
minutes. Right, they said to me, you've had your meal, get
off out of it. Meal? I said, what do you think I am, a dog?
Nothing better than a dog. What do you think I am, a wild
animal? What about them shoes I come all the way here to
get I heard you was giving away? I've a good mind to report
you to your mother superior. One of them, an Irish hooligan,
come at me. I cleared out. I took a short cut to Watford and
picked up a pair there. Got onto the North Circular, just
past Hendon, the sole come off, right where I was walking.
Lucky I had my old ones wrapped up, still carrying them,
otherwise I'd have been finished, man. So I've had to stay
with these, you see, they're gone, they're no good, all the
good's gone out of them.

ASTON. Try these.

    DAVIES *takes the shoes, takes off his sandals and tries them
on.*

DAVIES. Not a bad pair of shoes. (*He trudges round the room.*)
They're strong, all right. Yes. Not a bad shape of shoe.
This leather's hardy, en't? Very hardy. Some bloke tried to
flog me some suede the other day. I wouldn't wear them.
Can't beat leather, for wear. Suede goes off, it creases, it
stains for life in five minutes. You can't beat leather. Yes.
Good shoe this.

ASTON. Good.

    DAVIES *waggles his feet.*

DAVIES. Don't fit though.

ASTON. Oh?

DAVIES. No. I got a very broad foot.

ASTON. Mmnn.

DAVIES. These are too pointed, you see.

ASTON. Ah.

DAVIES. They'd cripple me in a week. I mean these ones I got on, they're no good but at least they're comfortable. Not much cop, but I mean they don't hurt. (*He takes them off and gives them back*). Thanks anyway, mister.

ASTON. I'll see what I can look out for you.

DAVIES. Good luck. I can't go on like this. Can't get from one place to another. And I'll have to be moving about, you see, try to get fixed up.

ASTON. Where you going to go?

DAVIES. Oh, I got one or two things in mind. I'm waiting for the weather to break.

Pause.

ASTON (*attending to the toaster*). Would . . . would you like to sleep here?

DAVIES. Here?

ASTON. You can sleep here if you like.

DAVIES. Here? Oh, I don't know about that.

Pause.

How long for?

ASTON. Till you . . . get yourself fixed up.

DAVIES (*sitting*). Ay well, that. . . .

ASTON. Get yourself sorted out. . . .

DAVIES. Oh, I'll be fixed up . . . pretty soon now. . . .

Pause.

Where would I sleep?

ASTON. Here. The other rooms would . . . would be no good to you.

DAVIES (*rising, looking about*). Here? Where?

ASTON (*rising, pointing upstage right*). There's a bed behind all that.

DAVIES. Oh, I see. Well, that's handy. Well, that's . . . I tell you what, I might do that . . . just till I get myself sorted out. You got enough furniture here.

ASTON. I picked it up. Just keeping it here for the time being. Thought it might come in handy.

DAVIES. This gas stove work, do it?

ASTON. No.

DAVIES. What do you do for a cup of tea?

ASTON. Nothing.

DAVIES. That's a bit rough. (DAVIES *observes the planks.*) You building something?

ASTON. I might build a shed out the back.

DAVIES. Carpenter, eh? (*He turns to the lawn-mower.*) Got a lawn.

ASTON. Have a look.

ASTON *lifts the sack at the window. They look out.*

DAVIES. Looks a bit thick.

ASTON. Overgrown.

DAVIES. What's that, a pond?

ASTON. Yes.

DAVIES. What you got, fish?

ASTON. No. There isn't anything in there.

Pause.

DAVIES. Where you going to put your shed?

ASTON (*turning*). I'll have to clear the garden first.

DAVIES. You'd need a tractor, man.

ASTON. I'll get it done.

DAVIES. Carpentry, eh?

ASTON (*standing still*). I like . . . working with my hands.

DAVIES *picks up the statue of Buddha.*

DAVIES. What's this?

ASTON (*taking and studying it*). That's a Buddha.

DAVIES. Get on.

ASTON. Yes. I quite like it. Picked it up in a . . . in a shop. Looked quite nice to me. Don't know why. What do you think of these Buddhas?

DAVIES. Oh, they're . . . they're all right, en't they?

ASTON. Yes, I was pleased when I got hold of this one. It's very well made.

DAVIES *turns and peers under the sink.*

DAVIES. This the bed here, is it?

ASTON (*moving to the bed*). We'll get rid of all that. The ladder'll fit under the bed. (*They put the ladder under the bed.*)

DAVIES (*indicating the sink*). What about this?

ASTON. I think that'll fit in under here as well.

DAVIES. I'll give you a hand. (*They lift it.*) It's a ton weight, en't?

ASTON. Under here.

DAVIES. This in use at all, then?

ASTON. No. I'll be getting rid of it. Here.
     They place the sink under the bed.
There's a lavatory down the landing. It's got a sink in there. We can put this stuff over there.

They begin to move the coal bucket, shopping trolley, lawn-mower and sideboard drawers to the right wall.

DAVIES (*stopping*). You don't share it, do you?

ASTON. What?

DAVIES. I mean you don't share the toilet with them Blacks, do you?

ASTON. They live next door.

DAVIES. They don't come in?
     ASTON puts a drawer against the wall.
Because, you know . . . I mean . . . fair's fair. . . .

ASTON goes to the bed, blows dust and shakes a blanket.

ASTON. You see a blue case?

DAVIES. Blue case? Down here. Look. By the carpet.
     ASTON goes to the case, opens it, takes out a sheet and pillow and puts them on the bed.
That's a nice sheet.

ASTON. The blanket'll be a bit dusty.

DAVIES. Don't you worry about that.

ASTON stands upright, takes out his tobacco and begins to roll a cigarette. He goes to his bed and sits.

ASTON. How are you off for money?

DAVIES. Oh well . . . now, mister, if you want the truth . . I'm a bit short.

ASTON takes some coins from his pocket, sorts them, and holds out five shillings.

ASTON. Here's a few bob.

DAVIES (*taking the coins*). Thank you, thank you, good luck. I just happen to find myself a bit short. You see, I got nothing for all that week's work I did last week. That's the position, that's what it is.

Pause.

ASTON. I went into a pub the other day. Ordered a Guinness. They gave it to me in a thick mug. I sat down but I couldn't drink it. I can't drink Guinness from a thick mug. I only like it out of a thin glass. I had a few sips but I couldn't finish it.

ASTON picks up a screwdriver and plug from the bed and begins to poke the plug.

DAVIES (*with great feeling*). If only the weather would break! Then I'd be able to get down to Sidcup!

ASTON. Sidcup?

DAVIES. The weather's so blasted bloody awful, how can I get down to Sidcup in these shoes?

ASTON. Why do you want to get down to Sidcup?

DAVIES. I got my papers there!

Pause.

ASTON. Your what?

DAVIES. I got my papers there!

Pause.

ASTON. What are they doing at Sidcup?

DAVIES. A man I know has got them. I left them with him.
You see? They prove who I am! I can't move without them
papers. They tell you who I am. You see! I'm stuck without
them.

ASTON. Why's that?

DAVIES. You see, what it is, you see, I changed my name!
Years ago. I been going around under an assumed name!
That's not my real name.

ASTON. What name you been going under?

DAVIES. Jenkins. Bernard Jenkins. That's my name. That's
the name I'm known, anyway. But it's no good me going on
with that name. I got no rights. I got an insurance card here.
(*He takes a card from his pocket.*) Under the name of Jenkins.
See? Bernard Jenkins. Look. It's got four stamps on it. Four
of them. But I can't go along with these. That's not my real
name, they'd find out, they'd have me in the nick. Four
stamps. I haven't paid out pennies. I've paid out pounds.
I've paid out pounds, not pennies. There's been other
stamps, plenty, but they haven't put them on, the nigs, I
never had enough time to go into it.

ASTON. They should have stamped your card.

DAVIES. It would have done no good! I'd have got nothing
anyway. That's not my real name. If I take that card along I
go in the nick.

ASTON. What's your real name, then?

DAVIES. Davies. Mac Davies. That was before I changed my
name.

   Pause.

ASTON. It looks as though you want to sort all that out.

DAVIES. If only I could get down to Sidcup! I've been waiting
for the weather to break. He's got my papers, this man I left
them with, it's got it all down there, I could prove everything.

ASTON. How long's he had them?

DAVIES. What?

ASTON. How long's he had them?

DAVIES. Oh, must be . . . it was in the war . . . must be
. . . about near on fifteen year ago.

He suddenly becomes aware of the bucket and looks up.

ASTON. Any time you want to . . . get into bed, just get in.
Don't worry about me.

DAVIES (*taking off his overcoat*). Eh, well, I think I will. I'm a
bit . . . a bit done in. (*He steps out of his trousers, and holds
them out*). Shall I put these on here?

ASTON. Yes.

DAVIES *puts the coat and trousers on the clothes horse.*

DAVIES. I see you got a bucket up here.

ASTON. Leak.

DAVIES *looks up.*

DAVIES. Well, I'll try your bed then. You getting in?

ASTON. I'm mending this plug.

DAVIES *looks at him and then at the gas stove.*

DAVIES. You . . . you can't move this, eh?

ASTON. Bit heavy.

DAVIES. Yes.

DAVIES *gets into bed. He tests his weight and length.*

Not bad. Not bad. A fair bed. I think I'll sleep in this.

ASTON. I'll have to fix a proper shade on that bulb. The
light's a bit glaring.

DAVIES. Don't you worry about that, mister, don't you worry
about that. (*He turns and puts the cover up*).

ASTON *sits, poking his plug.*
The LIGHTS FADE OUT. *Darkness.*
LIGHTS UP. *Morning.*
ASTON *is fastening his trousers, standing by the bed. He
straightens his bed. He turns, goes to the centre of the room*

and looks at DAVIES. *He turns, puts his jacket on, turns,*
goes towards DAVIES *and looks down on him.*
He coughs. DAVIES *sits up abruptly.*

DAVIES. What? What's this? What's this?

ASTON. It's all right.

DAVIES (*staring*). What's this?

ASTON. It's all right.

DAVIES *looks about.*

DAVIES. Oh, yes.

ASTON *goes to his bed, picks up the plug and shakes it.*

ASTON. Sleep well?

DAVIES. Yes. Dead out. Must have been dead out.

ASTON *goes downstage right, collects the toaster and*
examines it.

ASTON. You . . . er. . . .

DAVIES. Eh?

ASTON. Were you dreaming or something?

DAVIES. Dreaming?

ASTON. Yes.

DAVIES. I don't dream. I've never dreamed.

ASTON. No, nor have I.

DAVIES. Nor me.

Pause.

Why you ask me that, then?

ASTON. You were making noises.

DAVIES. Who was?

ASTON. You were.

DAVIES *gets out of bed. He wears long underpants.*

DAVIES. Now, wait a minute. Wait a minute, what do you
mean? What kind of noises?

ASTON. You were making groans. You were jabbering.

DAVIES. Jabbering? Me?

ASTON. Yes.

DAVIES. I don't jabber, man. Nobody ever told me that before.
>*Pause.*

What would I be jabbering about?

ASTON. I don't know.

DAVIES. I mean, where's the sense in it?
>*Pause.*

Nobody ever told me that before.
>*Pause.*

You got hold of the wrong bloke, mate.

ASTON (*crossing to the bed with the toaster*). No. You woke me
up. I thought you might have been dreaming.

DAVIES. I wasn't dreaming. I never had a dream in my life.

>*Pause.*

ASTON. Maybe it was the bed.

DAVIES. Nothing wrong with this bed.

ASTON. Might be a bit unfamiliar.

DAVIES. There's nothing unfamiliar about me with beds. I
slept in beds. I don't make noises just because I sleep in a
bed. I slept in plenty of beds.
>*Pause.*

I tell you what, maybe it were them Blacks.

ASTON. What?

DAVIES. Them noises.

ASTON. What Blacks?

DAVIES. Them you got. Next door. Maybe it were them Blacks
making noises, coming up through the walls.

ASTON. Hmmnn.

DAVIES. That's my opinion.

>ASTON *puts down the plug and moves to the door.*

Where you going, you going out?

ASTON. Yes.

DAVIES (*seizing the sandals*). Wait a minute then, just a minute.

ASTON. What you doing?

DAVIES (*putting on the sandals*). I better come with you.

ASTON. Why?

DAVIES. I mean, I better come out with you, anyway.

ASTON. Why?

DAVIES. Well . . . don't you want me to go out?

ASTON. What for?

DAVIES. I mean . . . when you're out. Don't you want me to get out . . . when you're out?

ASTON. You don't have to go out.

DAVIES. You mean . . . I can stay here?

ASTON. Do what you like. You don't have to come out just because I go out.

DAVIES. You don't mind me staying here?

ASTON. I've got a couple of keys. (*He goes to a box by his bed and finds them.*) This door and the front door. (*He hands them to* DAVIES.)

DAVIES. Thanks very much, the best of luck.

Pause. ASTON *stands.*

ASTON. I think I'll take a stroll down the road. A little . . . kind of a shop. Man there'd got a jig saw the other day. I quite liked the look of it.

DAVIES. A jig saw, mate?

ASTON. Yes. Could be very useful.

DAVIES. Yes.

Slight pause.

What's that then, exactly, then?

ASTON *walks up to the window and looks out.*

ASTON. A jig saw? Well, it comes from the same family as the fret saw. But it's an appliance, you see. You have to fix it on to a portable drill.

DAVIES. Ah, that's right. They're very handy.

ASTON. They are, yes.

Pause.

You know, I was sitting in a café the other day. I happened to be sitting at the same table as this woman. Well, we started to . . . we started to pick up a bit of a conversation. I don't know . . . about her holiday, it was, where she'd been. She'd been down to the south coast. I can't remember where though. Anyway, we were just sitting there, having this bit of a conversation . . . then suddenly she put her hand over to mine . . . and she said, how would you like me to have a look at your body?

DAVIES. Get out of it.

Pause.

ASTON. Yes. To come out with it just like that, in the middle of this conversation. Struck me as a bit odd.

DAVIES. They've said the same thing to me.

ASTON. Have they?

DAVIES. Women? There's many a time they've come up to me and asked me more or less the same question.

Pause.

ASTON. What did you say your name was?

DAVIES. Bernard Jenkins is my assumed one.

ASTON. No, your other one?

DAVIES. Davies. Mac Davies.

ASTON. Welsh, are you?

DAVIES. Eh?

ASTON. You Welsh?

Pause.

DAVIES. Well, I been around, you know . . . what I mean . . . I been about. . . .

ASTON. Where were you born then?

DAVIES. (*darkly*). What do you mean?

ASTON. Where were you born?

DAVIES. I was . . . uh . . . oh, it's a bit hard, like, to set your mind back . . . see what I mean . . . going back . . . . a good way . . . lose a bit of track, like . . . you know. . . .

ASTON (*going to below the fireplace*). See this plug? Switch it on here, if you like. This little fire.

DAVIES. Right, mister.

ASTON. Just plug in here.

DAVIES. Right, mister.

   ASTON *goes towards the door.*

   (*Anxiously*). What do I do?

ASTON. Just switch it on, that's all. The fire'll come on.

DAVIES. I tell you what. I won't bother about it.

ASTON. No trouble.

DAVIES. No, I don't go in for them things much.

ASTON. Should work. (*Turning*). Right.

DAVIES. Eh, I was going to ask you, mister, what about this stove? I mean, do you think it's going to be letting out any . . . what do you think?

ASTON. It's not connected.

DAVIES. You see, the trouble is, it's right on top of my bed, you see? What I got to watch is nudging . . . one of them gas taps with my elbow when I get up, you get my meaning?

He goes round to the other side of stove and examines it.

ASTON. There's nothing to worry about.

DAVIES. Now look here, don't you worry about it. All I'll do, I'll keep an eye on these taps every now and again, like, you see. See they're switched off. You leave it to me.

ASTON. I don't think . . . .

DAVIES (*coming round*). Eh, mister, just one thing . . . eh . . . . you couldn't slip me a couple of bob, for a cup of tea, just, you know?

ASTON. I gave you a few bob last night.

DAVIES. Eh, so you did. So you did. I forgot. Went clean out of my mind. That's right. Thank you, mister. Listen. You're sure now, you're sure you don't mind me staying here? I mean, I'm not the sort of man who wants to take any liberties.

ASTON. No, that's all right.

DAVIES. I might get down to Wembley later on in the day.

ASTON. Uh-uh.

DAVIES. There s a caff down there, you see, might be able to get fixed up there. I was there, see? I know they were a bit short-handed. They might be in the need of a bit of staff.

ASTON. When was that?

DAVIES. Eh? Oh, well, that was . . . near on . . . that'll be . . . that'll be a little while ago now. But of course what it is, they can't find the right kind of people in these places. What they want to do, they're trying to do away with these foreigners, you see, in catering. They want an Englishman to pour their tea, that's what they want, that's what they're crying out for. It's only common sense, en't? Oh, I got all that under way . . . that's . . . uh . . . that's . . . what I'll be doing.

> *Pause.*

If only I could get down there.

ASTON. Mmnn. (ASTON *moves to the door*.) Well, I'll be seeing you then.

DAVIES. Yes. Right.

> ASTON *goes out and closes the door.*
>
> DAVIES *stands still. He waits a few seconds, then goes to the door, opens it, looks out, closes it, stands with his back to it, turns swiftly, opens it, looks out, comes back, closes the door, finds the keys in his pocket, tries one, tries the other, locks the door. He looks about the room. He then goes quickly to* ASTON'S *bed, bends, brings out the pair of shoes and examines them.*

Not a bad pair of shoes. Bit pointed.

> *He puts them back under the bed. He examines the area by* ASTON'S *bed, picks up a vase and looks into it, then picks up a box and shakes it.*

Screws!

He sees paint buckets at the top of the bed, goes to them, and examines them.

Paint. What's he going to paint?

He puts the bucket down, comes to the centre of the room, looks up at bucket, and grimaces.

I'll have to find out about that. (*He crosses right, and picks up a blow-lamp.*) He's got some stuff in here. (*He picks up the Buddha and looks at it.*) Full of stuff. Look at all this. (*His eye falls on the piles of papers.*) What's he got all those papers for? Damn pile of papers.

He goes to a pile and touches it. The pile wobbles. He steadies it.

Hold it, hold it!

He holds the pile and pushes the papers back into place.
The door opens.

MICK *comes in, puts the key in his pocket, and closes the door silently. He stands at the door and watches* DAVIES.

What's he got all these papers for? (DAVIES *climbs over the rolled carpet to the blue case.*) Had a sheet and pillow ready in here. (*He opens the case.*) Nothing. (*He shuts the case.*) Still, I had a sleep though. I don't make no noises. (*He looks at the window.*) What's this?

He picks up another case and tries to open it. MICK *moves upstage, silently.*

Locked. (*He puts it down and moves downstage.*) Must be something in it. (*He picks up a sideboard drawer, rummages in the contents, then puts it down.*)

MICK *slides across the room.*

DAVIES *half turns,* MICK *seizes his arm and forces it up his back.* DAVIES *screams.*

Uuuuuuuhhh! Uuuuuuuhhh! What! What! What! Uuuuuuuhhh!

MICK *swiftly forces him to the floor, with* DAVIES *struggling, grimacing, whimpering and staring.*

MICK *holds his arm, puts his other hand to his lips, then puts his hand to* DAVIES' *lips.* DAVIES *quietens.* MICK *lets him go.* DAVIES *writhes.* MICK *holds out a warning finger. He then squats down to regard* DAVIES. *He regards him, then stands looking down on him.* DAVIES *massages his arm, watching* MICK. MICK *turns slowly to look at the room. He goes to* DAVIES' *bed and uncovers it. He turns, goes to the clothes horse and picks up* DAVIES' *trousers.* DAVIES *starts to rise.* MICK *presses him down with his foot and stands over him. Finally he removes his foot. He examines the trousers and throws them back.* DAVIES *remains on the floor, crouched.* MICK *slowly goes to the chair, sits, and watches* DAVIES, *expressionless.*

Silence.

MICK. What's the game?

Curtain.

Act Two

A few seconds later.

> MICK *is seated,* DAVIES *on the floor, half seated, crouched.*
> *Silence.*

MICK. Well?

DAVIES. Nothing, nothing. Nothing.

> *A drip sounds in the bucket overhead. They look up.* MICK
> *looks back to* DAVIES.

MICK. What's your name?

DAVIES. I don't know you. I don't know who you are.

> *Pause.*

MICK. Eh?

DAVIES. Jenkins.

MICK. Jenkins?

DAVIES. Yes.

MICK. Jen . . . kins.

> *Pause.*

You sleep here last night?

DAVIES. Yes.

MICK. Sleep well?

DAVIES. Yes.

MICK. I'm awfully glad. It's awfully nice to meet you.

> *Pause.*

What did you say your name was?

DAVIES. Jenkins.

MICK. I beg your pardon?

DAVIES. Jenkins!

> *Pause.*

MICK. Jen . . . kins.

A drip sounds in the bucket. DAVIES *looks up.*

You remind me of my uncle's brother. He was always on the move, that man. Never without his passport. Had an eye for the girls. Very much your build. Bit of an athlete. Long-jump specialist. He had a habit of demonstrating different run-ups in the drawing-room round about Christmas time. Had a penchant for nuts. That's what it was. Nothing else but a penchant. Couldn't eat enough of them. Peanuts, walnuts, brazil nuts, monkey nuts, wouldn't touch a piece of fruit cake. Had a marvellous stop-watch. Picked it up in Hong Kong. The day after they chucked him out of the Salvation Army. Used to go in number four for Beckenham Reserves. That was before he got his Gold Medal. Had a funny habit of carrying his fiddle on his back. Like a papoose. I think there was a bit of the Red Indian in him. To be honest, I've never made out how he came to be my uncle's brother. I've often thought that maybe it was the other way round. I mean that my uncle was his brother and he was my uncle. But I never called him uncle. As a matter of fact I called him Sid. My mother called him Sid too. It was a funny business. Your spitting image he was. Married a Chinaman and went to Jamaica.

Pause.

I hope you slept well last night.

DAVIES. Listen! I don't know who you are!

MICK. What bed you sleep in?

DAVIES. Now look here—

MICK. Eh?

DAVIES. That one.

MICK. Not the other one?

DAVIES. No.

MICK. Choosy.

Pause.

How do you like my room?

DAVIES. Your room?

MICK. Yes.

DAVIES. This ain't your room. I don't know who you are. I ain't never seen you before.

MICK. You know, believe it or not, you've got a funny kind of resemblance to a bloke I once knew in Shoreditch. Actually he lived in Aldgate. I was staying with a cousin in Camden Town. This chap, he used to have a pitch in Finsbury Park, just by the bus depot. When I got to know him I found out he was brought up in Putney. That didn't make any difference to me. I know quite a few people who were born in Putney. Even if they weren't born in Putney they were born in Fulham. The only trouble was, he wasn't born in Putney, he was only brought up in Putney. It turned out he was born in the Caledonian Road, just before you get to the Nag's Head. His old mum was still living at the Angel. All the buses passed right by the door. She could get a 38, 581, 30 or 38A, take her down the Essex Road to Dalston Junction in next to no time. Well, of course, if she got the 30 he'd take her up Upper Street way, round by Highbury Corner and down to St. Paul's Church, but she'd get to Dalston Junction just the same in the end. I used to leave my bike in her garden on my way to work. Yes, it was a curious affair. Dead spit of you he was. Bit bigger round the nose but there was nothing in it.

Pause.

Did you sleep here last night?

DAVIES. Yes.

MICK. Sleep well?

DAVIES. Yes!

MICK. Did you have to get up in the night?

DAVIES. No!

Pause.

MICK. What's your name?

DAVIES (*shifting, about to rise*). Now look here!

MICK. What?

DAVIES. Jenkins!

MICK. Jen . . . kins.

> DAVIES *makes a sudden move to rise. A violent bellow from* MICK *sends him back.*

(*A shout.*) Sleep here last night?

DAVIES. Yes. . . .

MICK (*continuing at great pace*). How'd you sleep?

DAVIES. I slept—

MICK. Sleep well?

DAVIES. Now look—

MICK. What bed?

DAVIES. That—

MICK. Not the other?

DAVIES. No!

MICK. Choosy.

> Pause.

(*Quietly.*) Choosy.

> Pause.

(*Again amiable.*) What sort of sleep did you have in that bed?

DAVIES (*banging on floor*). All right!

MICK. You weren't uncomfortable?

DAVIES (*groaning*). All right!

> MICK *stands, and moves to him.*

MICK. You a foreigner?

DAVIES. No.

MICK. Born and bred in the British Isles?

DAVIES. I was!

MICK. What did they teach you?

> Pause.

How did you like my bed?

> Pause.

That's my bed. You want to mind you don't catch a draught.

DAVIES. From the bed?

MICK. No, now, up your arse.

> DAVIES *stares warily at* MICK, *who turns.* DAVIES
> *scrambles to the clothes horse and seizes his trousers.* MICK
> *turns swiftly and grabs them.* DAVIES *lunges for them.*
> MICK *holds out a hand warningly.*

You intending to settle down here?

DAVIES. Give me my trousers then.

MICK. You settling down for a long stay?

DAVIES. Give me my bloody trousers!

MICK. Why, where you going?

DAVIES. Give me and I'm going, I'm going to Sidcup!

> MICK *flicks the trousers in* DAVIES' *face several times.*
> DAVIES *retreats.*
> *Pause.*

MICK. You know, you remind me of a bloke I bumped into
once, just the other side of the Guildford by-pass—

DAVIES. I was brought here!

> *Pause.*

MICK. Pardon?

DAVIES. I was brought here! I was brought here!

MICK. Brought here? Who brought you here?

DAVIES. Man who lives here . . . he. . . .

> *Pause.*

MICK. Fibber.

DAVIES. I was brought here, last night . . . met him in a
caff . . . I was working . . . I got the bullet . . . I was
working there . . . bloke saved me from a punch up,
brought me here, brought me right here.

> *Pause.*

MICK. I'm afraid you're a born fibber, en't you? You're
speaking to the owner. This is my room. You're standing
in my house.

DAVIES. It's his . . . he seen me all right . . . he. . . .

MICK (*pointing to* DAVIES' *bed*). That's my bed.

DAVIES. What about that, then?

MICK. That's my mother's bed.

DAVIES. Well she wasn't in it last night!

MICK (*moving to him*). Now don't get perky, son, don't get perky. Keep your hands off my old mum.

DAVIES. I ain't . . . I haven't. . . .

MICK. Don't get out of your depth, friend, don't start taking liberties with my old mother, let's have a bit of respect.

DAVIES. I got respect, you won't find anyone with more respect.

MICK. Well, stop telling me all these fibs.

DAVIES. Now listen to me, I never seen you before, have I?

MICK. Never seen my mother before either, I suppose?
    Pause.
I think I'm coming to the conclusion that you're an old rogue. You're nothing but an old scoundrel.

DAVIES. Now wait—

MICK. Listen, son. Listen, sonny. You stink.

DAVIES. You ain't got no right to—

MICK. You're stinking the place out. You're an old robber, there's no getting away from it. You're an old skate. You don't belong in a nice place like this. You're an old barbarian. Honest. You got no business wandering about in an unfurnished flat. I could charge seven quid a week for this if I wanted to. Get a taker tomorrow. Three hundred and fifty a year exclusive. No argument. I mean, if that sort of money's in your range don't be afraid to say so. Here you are. Furniture and fittings, I'll take four hundred or the nearest offer. Rateable value ninety quid for the annum. You can reckon water, heating and lighting at close on fifty. That'll cost you eight hundred and ninety if you're all that keen. Say the word and I'll have my solicitors draft you out a contract. Otherwise I've got the van outside, I can run you

to the police station in five minutes, have you in for tres-
passing, loitering with intent, daylight robbery, filching,
thieving and stinking the place out. What do you say?
Unless you're really keen on a straightforward purchase. Of
course, I'll get my brother to decorate it up for you first. I've
got a brother who's a number one decorator. He'll decorate
it up for you. If you want more space, there's four more
rooms along the landing ready to go. Bathroom, living-
room, bedroom and nursery. You can have this as your
study. This brother I mentioned, he's just about to start on
the other rooms. Yes, just about to start. So what do you
say? Eight hundred odd for this room or three thousand
down for the whole upper storey. On the other hand, if you
prefer to approach it in the long-term way I know an
insurance firm in West Ham'll be pleased to handle the
deal for you. No strings attached, open and above board,
untarnished record; twenty per cent interest, fifty per cent
deposit; down payments, back payments, family allowances,
bonus schemes, remission of term for good behaviour, six
months lease, yearly examination of the relevant archives,
tea laid on, disposal of shares, benefit extension, compen-
sation on cessation, comprehensive indemnity against Riot,
Civil Commotion, Labour Disturbances, Storm, Tempest,
Thunderbolt, Larceny or Cattle all subject to a daily check
and double check. Of course we'd need a signed declaration
from your personal medical attendant as assurance that you
possess the requisite fitness to carry the can, won't we?
Who do you bank with?

Pause.

Who do you bank with?

*The door opens. ASTON comes in. MICK turns and drops the
trousers. DAVIES picks them up and puts them on. ASTON,
after a glance at the other two, goes to his bed, places a bag
which he is carrying on it, sits down and resumes fixing the
toaster. DAVIES retreats to his corner. MICK sits in the chair.*

Silence.
A drip sounds in the bucket. They all look up.
Silence.

You still got that leak.

ASTON. Yes.

Pause.

It's coming from the roof.

MICK. From the roof, eh?

ASTON. Yes.

Pause.

I'll have to tar it over.

MICK. You're going to tar it over?

ASTON. Yes.

MICK. What?

ASTON. The cracks.

Pause.

MICK. You'll be tarring over the cracks on the roof.

ASTON. Yes.

Pause.

MICK. Think that'll do it?

ASTON. It'll do it, for the time being.

MICK. Uh.

Pause.

DAVIES (*abruptly*). What do you do—?
They both look at him.

What do you do . . . when that bucket's full?

Pause.

ASTON. Empty it.

Pause.

MICK. I was telling my friend you were about to start decorating the other rooms.

ASTON. Yes.

> *Pause.*

(*To* DAVIES.) I got your bag.

DAVIES. Oh. (*Crossing to him and taking it*). Oh thanks, mister, thanks. Give it to you, did they?

> DAVIES *crosses back with the bag.*
> MICK *rises and snatches it.*

MICK. What's this?

DAVIES. Give us it, that's my bag!

MICK (*warding him off*). I've seen this bag before.

DAVIES. That's my bag!

MICK (*eluding him*). This bag's very familiar.

DAVIES. What do you mean?

MICK. Where'd you get it?

ASTON (*rising, to them*). Scrub it.

DAVIES. That's mine.

MICK. Whose?

DAVIES. It's mine! Tell him it's mine!

MICK. This your bag?

DAVIES. Give me it!

ASTON. Give it to him.

MICK. What? Give him what?

DAVIES. That bloody bag!

MICK (*slipping it behind the gas stove*). What bag? (*To* DAVIES.) What bag?

DAVIES (*moving*). Look here!

MICK (*facing him*). Where you going?

DAVIES. I'm going to get . . . my old . . .

MICK. Watch your step, sonny! You're knocking at the door when no one's at home. Don't push it too hard. You come busting into a private house, laying your hands on anything you can lay your hands on. Don't overstep the mark, son.

> ASTON *picks up the bag.*

DAVIES. You thieving bastard ... you thieving skate ...
let me get my—

ASTON. Here you are. (ASTON *offers the bag to* DAVIES.)

> MICK *grabs it.* ASTON *takes it.*
>
> MICK *grabs it.* DAVIES *reaches for it.*
>
> ASTON *takes it.* MICK *reaches for it.*
>
> ASTON *gives it to* DAVIES. MICK *grabs it.*
>
> *Pause.*
>
> ASTON *takes it.* DAVIES *takes it.* MICK *takes it.* DAVIES
> *reaches for it.* ASTON *takes it.*
>
> *Pause.*
>
> ASTON *gives it to* MICK. MICK *gives it to* DAVIES.
>
> DAVIES *grasps it to him.*
>
> *Pause.*
>
> MICK *looks at* ASTON. DAVIES *moves away with the bag.*
> *He drops it.*
>
> *Pause.*
>
> *They watch him. He picks it up. Goes to his bed, and sits.*
> ASTON *goes to his bed, sits, and begins to roll a cigarette.*
> MICK *stands still.*
>
> *Pause.*
>
> *A drip sounds in the bucket. They all look up.*
>
> *Pause.*

How did you get on at Wembley?

DAVIES. Well, I didn't get down there.

> *Pause.*

No. I couldn't make it.

> MICK *goes to the door and exits.*

ASTON. I had a bit of bad luck with that jig saw. When I got
there it had gone.

> *Pause.*

DAVIES. Who was that feller?

ASTON. He's my brother.

DAVIES. Is he? He's a bit of a joker, en'he?

ASTON. Uh.

DAVIES. Yes . . . he's a real joker.

ASTON. He's got a sense of humour.

DAVIES. Yes, I noticed.

> *Pause.*

He's a real joker, that lad, you can see that.

> *Pause.*

ASTON. Yes, he tends . . . he tends to see the funny side of things.

DAVIES. Well, he's got a sense of humour, en' he?

ASTON. Yes.

DAVIES. Yes, you could tell that.

> *Pause.*

I could tell the first time I saw him he had his own way of looking at things.

> ASTON *stands, goes to the sideboard drawer, right, picks up the statue of Buddha, and puts it on the gas stove.*

ASTON. I'm supposed to be doing up the upper part of the house for him.

DAVIES. What . . . you mean . . . you mean it's his house?

ASTON. Yes. I'm supposed to be decorating this landing for him. Make a flat out of it.

DAVIES. What does he do, then?

ASTON. He's in the building trade. He's got his own van.

DAVIES. He don't live here, do he?

ASTON. Once I get that shed up outside . . . I'll be able to give a bit more thought to the flat, you see. Perhaps I can knock up one or two things for it. (*He walks to the window.*) I can work with my hands, you see. That's one thing I can do. I never knew I could. But I can do all sorts of things now, with my hands. You know, manual things. When I get that shed up out there . . . I'll have a workshop, you see. I . . . could do a bit of woodwork. Simple woodwork, to start. Working with . . . good wood.

Pause.

Of course, there's a lot to be done to this place. What I
think, though, I think I'll put in a partition . . . in one of
the rooms along the landing. I think it'll take it. You know
. . . they've got these screens . . . you know . . . Oriental.
They break up a room with them. Make it into two parts.
I could either do that or I could have a partition. I could
knock them up, you see, if I had a workshop.

Pause.

Anyway, I think I've decided on the partition.

Pause.

DAVIES. Eh, look here, I been thinking. This ain't my bag.

ASTON. Oh. No.

DAVIES. No, this ain't my bag. My bag, it was another kind of
bag altogether, you see. I know what they've done. What
they done, they kept my bag, and they given you another
one altogether.

ASTON. No . . . what happened was, someone had gone off
with your bag.

DAVIES (*rising*). That's what I said!

ASTON. Anyway, I picked that bag up somewhere else. It's got
a few . . . pieces of clothes in it too. He let me have the
whole lot cheap.

DAVIES (*opening the bag*). Any shoes?

DAVIES *takes two check shirts, bright red and bright green,
from the bag. He holds them up.*

Check.

ASTON. Yes.

DAVIES. Yes . . . well, I know about these sort of shirts,
you see. Shirts like these, they don't go far in the winter-
time. I mean, that's one thing I know for a fact. No, what
I need, is a kind of a shirt with stripes, a good solid shirt,
with stripes going down. That's what I want. (*He takes from
the bag a deep-red velvet smoking-jacket.*) What's this?

ASTON. It's a smoking-jacket.

DAVIES. A smoking-jacket? (*He feels it.*) This ain't a bad piece of cloth. I'll see how it fits.

He tries it on.

You ain't got a mirror here, have you?

ASTON. I don't think I have.

DAVIES. Well, it don't fit too bad. How do you think it looks?

ASTON. Looks all right.

DAVIES. Well, I won't say no to this, then.

ASTON *picks up the plug and examines it.*

No, I wouldn't say no to this.

Pause.

ASTON. You could be . . . caretaker here, if you liked.

DAVIES. What?

ASTON. You could . . . look after the place, if you liked . . . you know, the stairs and the landing, the front steps, keep an eye on it. Polish the bells.

DAVIES. Bells?

ASTON. I'll be fixing a few, down by the front door. Brass.

DAVIES. Caretaking, eh?

ASTON. Yes.

DAVIES. Well, I . . . I never done caretaking before, you know . . . I mean to say . . . I never . . . what I mean to say is . . . I never been a caretaker before.

Pause.

ASTON. How do you feel about being one, then?

DAVIES. Well, I reckon . . . Well, I'd have to know . . . you know. . . .

ASTON. What sort of. . . .

DAVIES. Yes, what sort of . . . you know. . . .

Pause.

ASTON. Well, I mean. . . .

DAVIES. I mean, I'd have to . . . I'd have to. . . .

ASTON. Well, I could tell you. . . .

DAVIES. That's . . . that's it . . . you see . . . you get my
meaning?

ASTON. When the time comes. . . .

DAVIES. I mean, that's what I'm getting at, you see. . . .

ASTON. More or less exactly what you. . . .

DAVIES. You see, what I mean to say . . . what I'm getting
at is . . . I mean, what sort of jobs. . . .

   Pause.

ASTON. Well, there's things like the stairs . . . and the . . .
the bells. . . .

DAVIES. But it'd be a matter . . . wouldn't it . . . it'd be a
matter of a broom . . . isn't it?

ASTON. Yes, and of course, you'd need a few brushes.

DAVIES. You'd need implements . . . you see . . . you'd
need a good few implements. . . .

   ASTON *takes a white overall from a nail over his bed, and
   shows it to* DAVIES.

ASTON. You could wear this, if you liked.

DAVIES. Well . . . that's nice, en't?

ASTON. It'd keep the dust off.

DAVIES (*putting it on*). Yes, this'd keep the dust off, all right.
Well off. Thanks very much, mister.

ASTON. You see, what we could do, we could . . . I could fit
a bell at the bottom, outside the front door, with "Caretaker"
on it. And you could answer any queries.

DAVIES. Oh, I don't know about that.

ASTON. Why not?

DAVIES. Well, I mean, you don't know who might come up
them front steps, do you? I got to be a bit careful.

ASTON. Why, someone after you?

DAVIES. After me? Well, I could have that Scotch git coming
looking after me, couldn't I? All I'd do, I'd hear the bell, I'd
go down there, open the door, who might be there, any Harry

might be there. I could be buggered as easy as that, man. They might be there after my card, I mean look at it, here I am, I only got four stamps, on this card, here it is, look, four stamps, that's all I got, I ain't got any more, that's all I got, they ring the bell called Caretaker, they'd have me in, that's what they'd do, I wouldn't stand a chance. Of course I got plenty of other cards lying about, but they don't know that, and I can't tell them, can I, because then they'd find out I was going about under an assumed name. You see, the name I call myself now, that's not my real name. My real name's not the one I'm using, you see. It's different. You see, the name I go under now ain't my real one. It's assumed.

Silence.
THE LIGHTS FADE TO BLACKOUT.
THEN UP TO DIM LIGHT THROUGH THE WINDOW.
A door bangs.
Sound of a key in the door of the room.
DAVIES *enters, closes the door, and tries the light switch, on, off, on, off.*

DAVIES (*muttering*). What's this? (*He switches on and off.*) What's the matter with this damn light? (*He switches on and off.*) Aaah. Don't tell me the damn light's gone now.
Pause.
What'll I do? Damn light's gone now. Can't see a thing.
Pause.
What'll I do now? (*He moves, stumbles.*) Ah God, what's that? Give me a light. Wait a minute.
He feels for matches in his pocket, takes out a box and lights one. The match goes out. The box falls.
Aah! Where is it? (*Stooping.*) Where's the bloody box?
The box is kicked.
What's that? What? Who's that? What's that?
Pause. He moves.

Where's my box? It was down here. Who's this? Who's
moving it?
Silence.
Come on. Who's this? Who's this got my box?
Pause.
Who's in here!
Pause.
I got a knife here. I'm ready. Come on then, who are you?
He moves, stumbles, falls and cries out.
Silence.
A faint whimper from DAVIES. *He gets up.*
All right!
He stands. Heavy breathing.
*Suddenly the electrolux starts to hum. A figure moves with it,
guiding it. The nozzle moves along the floor after* DAVIES,
who skips, dives away from it and falls, breathlessly.
Ah, ah, ah, ah, ah, ah! Get away-y-y-y-y!
The electrolux stops. The figure jumps on ASTON'S *bed.*
I'm ready for you! I'm . . . I'm . . . I'm here!

*The figure takes out the electrolux plug from the light socket
and fits the bulb. The light goes on.* DAVIES *flattens himself
against right wall, knife in hand.* MICK *stands on the bed,
holding the plug.*

MICK. I was just doing some spring cleaning. (*He gets down.*)
There used to be a wall plug for this electrolux. But it
doesn't work. I had to fit it in the light socket. (*He puts the
electrolux under* ASTON'S *bed.*) How do you think the place
is looking? I gave it a good going over.
Pause.
We take it in turns, once a fortnight, my brother and me, to
give the place a thorough going over. I was working late tonight, I only just got here. But I thought I better get on with
it, as it's my turn.

Pause.

It's not that I actually live here. I don't. As a matter of fact I live somewhere else. But after all, I'm responsible for the upkeep of the premises, en' I? Can't help being house-proud.

He moves towards DAVIES *and indicates the knife.*

What are you waving that about for?

DAVIES. You come near me. . . .

MICK. I'm sorry if I gave you a start. But I had you in mind too, you know. I mean, my brother's guest. We got to think of your comfort, en't we? Don't want the dust to get up your nose. How long you thinking of staying here, by the way? As a matter of fact, I was going to suggest that we'd lower your rent, make it just a nominal sum, I mean until you get fixed up. Just nominal, that's all.

Pause.

Still, if you're going to be spiky, I'll have to reconsider the whole proposition.

Pause.

Eh, you're not thinking of doing any violence on me, are you? You're not the violent sort, are you?

DAVIES (*vehemently*). I keep myself to myself, mate. But if anyone starts with me though, they know what they got coming.

MICK. I can believe that.

DAVIES. You do. I been all over, see? You understand my meaning? I don't mind a bit of a joke now and then, but anyone'll tell you . . . that no one starts anything with me.

MICK. I get what you mean, yes.

DAVIES. I can be pushed so far . . . but. . . .

MICK. No further.

DAVIES. That's it.

MICK sits on junk down right.

What you doing?

MICK. No, I just want to say that . . . I'm very impressed
  by that.

DAVIES. Eh?

MICK. I'm very impressed by what you've just said.
    Pause.
  Yes, that's impressive, that is.
    Pause.
  I'm impressed, anyway.

DAVIES. You know what I'm talking about then?

MICK. Yes, I know. I think we understand one another.

DAVIES. Uh? Well . . . I'll tell you . . . I'd . . . I'd like
  to think that. You been playing me about, you know. I don't
  know why. I never done you no harm.

MICK. No, you know what it was? We just got off on the wrong
  foot. That's all it was.

DAVIES. Ay, we did.

    DAVIES *joins* MICK *in junk.*

MICK. Like a sandwich?

DAVIES. What?

MICK (*taking a sandwich from his pocket*). Have one of these.

DAVIES. Don't you pull anything.

MICK. No, you're still not understanding me. I can't help
  being interested in any friend of my brother's. I mean,
  you're my brother's friend, aren't you?

DAVIES. Well, I . . . I wouldn't put it as far as that.

MICK. Don't you find him friendly, then?

DAVIES. Well, I wouldn't say we was all that friends. I mean,
  he done me no harm, but I wouldn't say he was any particular friend of mine. What's in that sandwich, then?

MICK. Cheese.

DAVIES. That'll do me.

MICK. Take one.

DAVIES. Thank you, mister.

MICK. I'm sorry to hear my brother's not very friendly.

DAVIES. He's friendly, he's friendly, I didn't say he wasn't. . . .

MICK (*taking a salt-cellar from his pocket*). Salt?

DAVIES. No thanks. (*He munches the sandwich.*) I just can't exactly . . . make him out.

MICK (*feeling in his pocket*). I forgot the pepper.

DAVIES. Just can't get the hang of him, that's all.

MICK. I had a bit of beetroot somewhere. Must have mislaid it.

> *Pause.*
>
> DAVIES *chews the sandwich.* MICK *watches him eat. He then rises and strolls downstage.*

Uuh . . . listen . . . can I ask your advice? I mean, you're a man of the world. Can I ask your advice about something?

DAVIES. You go right ahead.

MICK. Well, what it is, you see, I'm . . . I'm a bit worried about my brother.

DAVIES. Your brother?

MICK. Yes . . . you see, his trouble is. . . .

DAVIES. What?

MICK. Well, it's not a very nice thing to say. . . .

DAVIES (*rising, coming downstage*). Go on now, you say it.

> MICK *looks at him.*

MICK. He doesn't like work.

> *Pause.*

DAVIES. Go on!

MICK. No, he just doesn't like work, that's his trouble.

DAVIES. Is that a fact?

MICK. It's a terrible thing to have to say about your own brother.

DAVIES. Ay.

MICK. He's just shy of it. Very shy of it.

DAVIES. I know that sort.

MICK. You know the type?

DAVIES. I've met them.

MICK. I mean, I want to get him going in the world.

DAVIES. Stands to reason, man.

MICK. If you got an older brother you want to push him on, you want to see him make his way. Can't have him idle, he's only doing himself harm. That's what I say.

DAVIES. Yes.

MICK. But he won't buckle down to the job.

DAVIES. He don't like work.

MICK. Work shy.

DAVIES. Sounds like it to me.

MICK. You've met the type, have you?

DAVIES. Me? I know that sort.

MICK. Yes.

DAVIES. I know that sort. I've met them.

MICK. Causing me great anxiety. You see, I'm a working man: I'm a tradesman. I've got my own van.

DAVIES. Is that a fact?

MICK. He's supposed to be doing a little job for me . . . I keep him here to do a little job . . . but I don't know . . . I'm coming to the conclusion he's a slow worker.

 Pause.

What would your advice be?

DAVIES. Well . . . he's a funny bloke, your brother.

MICK. What?

DAVIES. I was saying, he's . . . he's a bit of a funny bloke, your brother.

 MICK *stares at him.*

MICK. Funny? Why?

DAVIES. Well . . . he's funny. . . .

MICK. What's funny about him?

 Pause.

DAVIES. Not liking work.

MICK. What's funny about that?

DAVIES. Nothing.

> *Pause.*

MICK. I don't call it funny.

DAVIES. Nor me.

MICK. You don't want to start getting hypercritical.

DAVIES. No, no, I wasn't that, I wasn't . . . I was only saying. . . .

MICK. Don't get too glib.

DAVIES. Look, all I meant was—

MICK. Cut it! (*Briskly.*) Look! I got a proposition to make to you. I'm thinking of taking over the running of this place, you see? I think it could be run a bit more efficiently. I got a lot of ideas, a lot of plans. (*He eyes* DAVIES.) How would you like to stay on here, as caretaker?

DAVIES. What?

MICK. I'll be quite open with you. I could rely on a man like you around the place, keeping an eye on things.

DAVIES. Well now . . . wait a minute . . . I . . . I ain't never done no caretaking before, you know. . . .

MICK. Doesn't matter about that. It's just that you look a capable sort of man to me.

DAVIES. I am a capable sort of man. I mean to say, I've had plenty offers in my time, you know, there's no getting away from that.

MICK. Well, I could see before, when you took out that knife, that you wouldn't let anyone mess you about.

DAVIES. No one messes me about, man.

MICK. I mean, you've been in the services, haven't you?

DAVIES. The what?

MICK. You been in the services. You can tell by your stance.

DAVIES. Oh . . . yes. Spent half my life there, man. Overseas . . . like . . . serving . . . I was.

MICK. In the colonies, weren't you?

DAVIES. I was over there. I was one of the first over there.

MICK. That's it. You're just the man I been looking for.

DAVIES. What for?

MICK. Caretaker.

DAVIES. Yes, well . . . look . . . listen . . . who's the landlord here, him or you?

MICK. Me. I am. I got deeds to prove it.

DAVIES. Ah . . . (*Decisively.*) Well listen, I don't mind doing a bit of caretaking, I wouldn't mind looking after the place for you.

MICK. Of course, we'd come to a small financial agreement, mutually beneficial.

DAVIES. I leave you to reckon that out, like.

MICK. Thanks. There's only one thing.

DAVIES. What's that?

MICK. Can you give me any references?

DAVIES. Eh?

MICK. Just to satisfy my solicitor.

DAVIES. I got plenty of references. All I got to do is to go down to Sidcup tomorrow. I got all the references I want down there.

MICK. Where's that?

DAVIES. Sidcup. He ain't only got my references down there, he got all my papers down there. I know that place like the back of my hand. I'm going down there anyway, see what I mean, I got to get down there, or I'm done.

MICK. So we can always get hold of these references if we want them.

DAVIES. I'll be down there any day, I tell you. I was going down today, but I'm . . . I'm waiting for the weather to break.

MICK. Ah.

DAVIES. Listen. You can't pick me up a pair of good shoes, can you? I got a bad need for a good pair of shoes. I can't get anywhere without a pair of good shoes, see? Do you think there's any chance of you being able to pick me up a pair?

THE LIGHTS FADE TO BLACKOUT.
LIGHTS UP. *Morning.*
ASTON *is pulling on his trousers over long underwear. A slight grimace. He looks around at the head of his bed, takes a towel from the rail and waves it about. He pulls it down, goes to* DAVIES *and wakes him.* DAVIES *sits up abruptly.*

ASTON. You said you wanted me to get you up.

DAVIES. What for?

ASTON. You said you were thinking of going to Sidcup.

DAVIES. Ay, that'd be a good thing, if I got there.

ASTON. Doesn't look much of a day.

DAVIES. Ay, well, that's shot it, en't it?

ASTON. I . . . I didn't have a very good night again.

DAVIES. I slept terrible.

Pause.

ASTON. You were making. . . .

DAVIES. Terrible. Had a bit of rain in the night, didn't it?

ASTON. Just a bit.

He goes to his bed, picks up a small plank and begins to sand-paper it.

DAVIES. Thought so. Come in on my head.
Pause.
Draught's blowing right in on my head, anyway.
Pause.
Can't you close that window behind that sack?

ASTON. You could.

DAVIES. Well then, what about it, then? The rain's coming right in on my head.

ASTON. Got to have a bit of air.

DAVIES *gets out of bed. He is wearing his trousers, waistcoat and vest.*

DAVIES (*putting on his sandals*). Listen. I've lived all my life in the air, boy. You don't have to tell me about air. What I'm saying is, there's too much air coming in that window when I'm asleep.

ASTON. Gets very stuffy in here without that window open.

> ASTON *crosses to the chair, puts the plank on it, and continues sandpapering.*

DAVIES. Yes, but listen, you don't know what I'm telling you. That bloody rain, man, come right in on my head. Spoils my sleep. I could catch my death of cold with it, with that draught. That's all I'm saying. Just shut that window and no one's going to catch any colds, that's all I'm saying.

> *Pause.*

ASTON. I couldn't sleep in here without that window open.

DAVIES. Yes, but what about me? What . . . what you got to say about my position?

ASTON. Why don't you sleep the other way round?

DAVIES. What do you mean?

ASTON. Sleep with your feet to the window.

DAVIES. What good would that do?

ASTON. The rain wouldn't come in on your head.

DAVIES. No, I couldn't do that. I couldn't do that.

> *Pause.*

I mean, I got used to sleeping this way. It isn't me has to change, it's that window. You see, it's raining now. Look at it. It's coming down now.

> *Pause.*

ASTON. I think I'll have a walk down to Goldhawk Road. I got talking to a man there. He had a saw bench. It looked in pretty good condition to me. Don't think it's much good to him.

> *Pause.*

Have a walk down there, I think.

DAVIES. Listen to that. That's done my trip to Sidcup. Eh, what about closing that window now? It'll be coming in here.

ASTON. Close it for the time being.

DAVIES *closes the window and looks out.*

DAVIES. What's all that under that tarpaulin out there?

ASTON. Wood.

DAVIES. What for?

ASTON. To build my shed.

DAVIES *sits on his bed.*

DAVIES. You haven't come across that pair of shoes you was going to look out for me, have you?

ASTON. Oh. No. I'll see if I can pick some up today.

DAVIES. I can't go out in this with these, can I? I can't even go out and get a cup of tea.

ASTON. There's a café just along the road.

DAVIES. There may be, mate.

During ASTON'S *speech the room grows darker.*
By the close of the speech only ASTON *can be seen clearly.*
DAVIES *and all the other objects are in the shadow. The fade-down of the light must be as gradual, as protracted and as unobtrusive as possible.*

ASTON. I used to go there quite a bit. Oh, years ago now. But I stopped. I used to like that place. Spent quite a bit of time in there. That was before I went away. Just before. I think that . . . place had a lot to do with it. They were all . . . a good bit older than me. But they always used to listen. I thought . . . they understood what I said. I mean I used to talk to them. I talked too much. That was my mistake. The same in the factory. Standing there, or in the breaks, I used to . . . talk about things. And these men, they used to listen, whenever I . . . had anything to say. It was all right. The trouble was, I used to have kind of hallucinations.

They weren't hallucinations, they . . . I used to get the
feeling I could see things . . . very clearly . . . everything . . .
was so clear . . . everything used . . . everything used to
get very quiet . . . everything got very quiet . . . all this
. . . quiet . . . and . . . this clear sight . . . it was
. . . but maybe I was wrong. Anyway, someone must have
said something. I didn't know anything about it. And . . .
some kind of lie must have got around. And this lie went
round. I thought people started being funny. In that café.
The factory. I couldn't understand it. Then one day they
took me to a hospital, right outside London. They . . . got
me there. I didn't want to go. Anyway . . . I tried to get
out, quite a few times. But . . . it wasn't very easy. They
asked me questions, in there. Got me in and asked me all
sorts of questions. Well, I told them . . . when they
wanted to know . . . what my thoughts were. Hmmnn.
Then one day . . . this man . . . doctor, I suppose . . .
the head one . . . he was quite a man of . . . distinction
. . . although I wasn't so sure about that. He called me in.
He said . . . he told me I had something. He said they'd
concluded their examination. That's what he said. And he
showed me a pile of papers and he said that I'd got something, some complaint. He said . . . he just said that, you
see. You've got . . . this thing. That's your complaint.
And we've decided, he said, that in your interests there's
only one course we can take. He said . . . but I can't
. . . exactly remember . . . how he put it . . . he said,
we're going to do something to your brain. He said . . . if
we don't, you'll be in here for the rest of your life, but if we
do, you stand a chance. You can go out, he said, and live like
the others. What do you want to do to my brain, I said to
him. But he just repeated what he'd said. Well, I wasn't a
fool. I knew I was a minor. I knew he couldn't do anything
to me without getting permission. I knew he had to get
permission from my mother. So I wrote to her and told her

what they were trying to do. But she signed their form, you
see, giving them permission. I know that because he showed
me her signature when I brought it up. Well, that night I
tried to escape, that night. I spent five hours sawing at one
of the bars on the window in this ward. Right throughout
the dark. They used to shine a torch over the beds every
half hour. So I timed it just right. And then it was nearly
done, and a man had a ... he had a fit, right next to me.
And they caught me, anyway. About a week later they
started to come round and do this thing to the brain. We
were all supposed to have it done, in this ward. And they
came round and did it one at a time. One a night. I was one
of the last. And I could see quite clearly what they did to the
others. They used to come round with these ... I don't
know what they were ... they looked like big pincers, with
wires on, the wires were attached to a little machine. It was
electric. They used to hold the man down, and this chief
... the chief doctor, used to fit the pincers, something like
earphones, he used to fit them on either side of the man's
skull. There was a man holding the machine, you see, and
he'd ... turn it on, and the chief would just press these
pincers on either side of the skull and keep them there.
Then he'd take them off. They'd cover the man up ...
and they wouldn't touch him again until later on. Some used
to put up a fight, but most of them didn't. They just lay
there. Well, they were coming round to me, and the night
they came I got up and stood against the wall. They told me
to get on the bed, and I knew they had to get me on the bed
because if they did it while I was standing up they might
break my spine. So I stood up and then one or two of them
came for me, well, I was younger then, I was much stronger
than I am now, I was quite strong then, I laid one of them
out and I had another one round the throat, and then
suddenly this chief had these pincers on my skull and I knew
he wasn't supposed to do it while I was standing up, that's

why I ..... anyway, he did it. So I did get out. I got
out of the place ... but I couldn't walk very well. I don't
think my spine was damaged. That was perfectly all right.
The trouble was ... my thoughts ... had become very
slow ... I couldn't think at all ... I couldn't ...
get ... my thoughts ... together ... uuuhh ... I
could ... never quite get it ... together. The trouble
was, I couldn't hear what people were saying. I couldn't
look to the right or the left, I had to look straight in front of
me, because if I turned my head round ... I couldn't
keep ... upright. And I had these headaches. I used to
sit in my room. That was when I lived with my mother. And
my brother. He was younger than me. And I laid everything out, in order, in my room, all the things I knew were
mine, but I didn't die. The thing is, I should have been
dead. I should have died. Anyway, I feel much better now.
But I don't talk to people now. I steer clear of places like
that café. I never go into them now. I don't talk to anyone
... like that. I've often thought of going back and trying
to find the man who did that to me. But I want to do something first. I want to build that shed out in the garden.

Curtain

Act Three

Two weeks later.

MICK is lying on the floor, down left, his head resting on the rolled carpet, looking up at the ceiling.

DAVIES is sitting in the chair, holding his pipe. He is wearing the smoking jacket. It is afternoon.

Silence.

DAVIES. I got a feeling he's done something to them cracks.

Pause.

See, there's been plenty of rain in the last week, but it ain't been dripping into the bucket.

Pause.

He must have tarred it over up there.

Pause.

There was someone walking about on the roof the other night. It must have been him.

Pause.

But I got a feeling he's tarred it over on the roof up there. Ain't said a word to me about it. Don't say a word to me.

Pause.

He don't answer me when I talk to him.

He lights a match, holds it to his pipe, and blows it.

He don't give me no knife!

Pause.

He don't give me no knife to cut my bread.

Pause.

How can I cut a loaf of bread without no knife?

Pause.

It's an impossibility.

Pause.

MICK. You've got a knife.

DAVIES. What?

MICK. You've got a knife.

DAVIES. I got a knife, sure I got a knife, but how do you
expect me to cut a good loaf of bread with that? That's not a
bread-knife. It's nothing to do with cutting bread. I picked
it up somewhere. I don't know where it's been, do I? No,
what I want—

MICK. I know what you want.

Pause. DAVIES *rises and goes to the gas stove.*

DAVIES. What about this gas stove? He tells me it's not connected. How do I know it's not connected? Here I am, I'm
sleeping right with it, I wake up in the middle of the night,
I'm looking right into the oven, man! It's right next to my
face, how do I know, I could be lying there in bed, it might
blow up, it might do me harm!

Pause.

But he don't seem to take any notice of what I say to him.
I told him the other day, see, I told him about them Blacks,
about them Blacks coming up from next door, and using the
lavatory. I told him, it was all dirty in there, all the banisters
were dirty, they were black, all the lavatory was black. But
what did he do? He's supposed to be in charge of it here, he
had nothing to say, he hadn't got a word to say.

Pause.

Couple of weeks ago . . . he sat there, he give me a long
chat . . . about a couple of weeks ago. A long chat he give
me. Since then he ain't said hardly a word. He went on
talking there . . . I don't know what he was . . . he
wasn't looking at me, he wasn't talking to me, he don't care
about me. He was talking to himself! That's all he worries
about. I mean, you come up to me, you ask my advice, he

wouldn't never do a thing like that. I mean, we don't have
any conversation, you see? You can't live in the same room
with someone who . . . who don't have any conversation
with you.

    Pause.

I just can't get the hang of him.

    Pause.

You and me, we could get this place going.

MICK (*ruminatively*). Yes, you're quite right. Look what I
could do with this place.

    Pause.

I could turn this place into a penthouse. For instance . . .
this room. This room you could have as the kitchen. Right
size, nice window, sun comes in. I'd have . . . I'd have
teal-blue, copper and parchment linoleum squares. I'd have
those colours re-echoed in the walls. I'd offset the kitchen
units with charcoal-grey worktops. Plenty of room for cupboards for the crockery. We'd have a small wall cupboard, a
large wall cupboard, a corner wall cupboard with revolving
shelves. You wouldn't be short of cupboards. You could put
the dining-room across the landing, see? Yes. Venetian
blinds on the window, cork floor, cork tiles. You could
have an off-white pile linen rug, a table in . . . in afromosia
teak veneer, sideboard with matt black drawers, curved
chairs with cushioned seats, armchairs in oatmeal tweed,
a beech frame settee with a woven sea-grass seat, white-
topped heat-resistant coffee table, white tile surround. Yes.
Then the bedroom. What's a bedroom? It's a retreat. It's a
place to go for rest and peace. So you want quiet decoration.
The lighting functional. Furniture . . . mahogany and
rosewood. Deep azure-blue carpet, unglazed blue and white
curtains, a bedspread with a pattern of small blue roses on a
white ground, dressing-table with a lift-up top containing a
plastic tray, table lamp of white raffia . . . (MICK *sits up.*)
it wouldn't be a flat it'd be a palace.

DAVIES. I'd say it would, man.

MICK. A palace.

DAVIES. Who would live there?

MICK. I would. My brother and me.

Pause.

DAVIES. What about me?

MICK (*quietly*). All this junk here, it's no good to anyone. It's just a lot of old iron, that's all. Clobber. You couldn't make a home out of this. There's no way you could arrange it. It's junk. He could never sell it, either, he wouldn't get tuppence for it.

Pause.

Junk.

Pause.

But he doesn't seem to be interested in what I got in mind, that's the trouble. Why don't you have a chat with him, see if he's interested?

DAVIES. Me?

MICK. Yes. You're a friend of his.

DAVIES. He's no friend of mine.

MICK. You're living in the same room with him, en't you?

DAVIES. He's no friend of mine. You don't know where you are with him. I mean, with a bloke like you, you know where you are.

MICK looks at him.

I mean, you get your own ways, I'm not saying you ain't got your own ways, anyone can see that. You may have some funny ways, but that's the same with all of us, but with him it's different, see? I mean at least with you, the thing with you is you're . . .

MICK. Straightforward.

DAVIES. That's it, you're straightforward.

MICK. Yes.

DAVIES. But with him, you don't know what he's up to half the time!

MICK. Uh.

DAVIES. He's got no feelings!

Pause.

See, what I need is a clock! I need a clock to tell the time! How can I tell the time without a clock? I can't do it! I said to him, I said, look here, what about getting in a clock, so's I can tell what time it is? I mean, if you can't tell what time you're at you don't know where you are, you understand my meaning? See, what I got to do now, if I'm walking about outside, I got to get my eye on a clock, and keep the time in my head for when I come in. But that's no good, I mean I'm not in here five minutes and I forgotten it. I forgotten what time it was!

DAVIES *walks up and down the room.*

Look at it this way. If I don't feel well I have a bit of a lay down, then, when I wake up, I don't know what time it is to go and have a cup of tea! You see, it's not so bad when I'm coming in. I can see the clock on the corner, the moment I'm stepping into the house I know what the time is, but when I'm *in*! It's when I'm *in* . . . that I haven't the foggiest idea what time it is!

Pause.

No, what I need is a clock in here, in this room, and then I stand a bit of a chance. But he don't give me one.

DAVIES *sits in the chair.*

He wakes me up! He wakes me up in the middle of the night! Tells me I'm making noises! I tell you I've half a mind to give him a mouthful one of these days.

MICK. He don't let you sleep?

DAVIES. He don't let me sleep! He wakes me up!

MICK. That's terrible.

DAVIES. I been plenty of other places. They always let

me sleep. It's the same the whole world over. Except here.

MICK. Sleep's essential. I've always said that.

DAVIES. You're right, it's essential. I get up in the morning, I'm worn out! I got business to see to. I got to move myself, I got to sort myself out, I got to get fixed up. But when I wake up in the morning, I ain't got no energy in me. And on top of that I ain't got no clock.

MICK. Yes.

DAVIES (*standing, moving*). He goes out, I don't know where he goes to, where's he go, he never tells me. We used to have a bit of a chat, not any more. I never see him, he goes out, he comes in late, next thing I know he's shoving me about in the middle of the night.

    Pause.

Listen! I wake up in the morning . . . I wake up in the morning and he's smiling at me! He's standing there, looking at me, smiling! I can see him, you see, I can see him through the blanket. He puts on his coat, he turns himself round, he looks down at my bed, there's a smile on his face! What the hell's he smiling at? What he don't know is that I'm watching him through that blanket. He don't know that! He don't know I can see him, he thinks I'm asleep, but I got my eye on him all the time through the blanket, see? But he don't know that! He just looks at me and he smiles, but he don't know that I can see him doing it!

    Pause.

(*Bending, close to* MICK.) No, what you want to do, you want to speak to him, see? I got . . . I got that worked out. You want to tell him . . . that we got ideas for this place, we could build it up, we could get it started. You see, I could decorate it out for you, I could give you a hand in doing it . . . between us.

    Pause.

Where do you live now, then?

MICK. Me? Oh, I've got a little place. Not bad. Everything

laid on. You must come up and have a drink some time. Listen to some Tchaikovsky.

DAVIES. No, you see, you're the bloke who wants to talk to him. I mean, you're his brother.

Pause.

MICK. Yes . . . maybe I will.

A door bangs.
MICK *rises, goes to the door and exits.*

DAVIES. Where you going? This is him!

Silence.
DAVIES *stands, then goes to the window and looks out.*
ASTON *enters. He is carrying a paper bag. He takes off his overcoat, opens the bag and takes out a pair of shoes.*

ASTON. Pair of shoes.

DAVIES (*turning*). What?

ASTON. I picked them up. Try them.

DAVIES. Shoes? What sort?

ASTON. They might do you.

DAVIES *comes down stage, takes off his sandals and tries the shoes on. He walks about, waggling his feet, bends, and presses the leather.*

DAVIES. No, they're not right.

ASTON. Aren't they?

DAVIES. No, they don't fit.

ASTON. Mmnn.

Pause.

DAVIES. Well, I'll tell you what, they might do . . . until I get another pair.

Pause.

Where's the laces?

ASTON. No laces.

DAVIES. I can't wear them without laces.

ASTON. I just got the shoes.

DAVIES. Well now, look that puts the lid on it, don't it?
I mean, you couldn't keep these shoes on right without a
pair of laces. The only way to keep a pair of shoes on, if you
haven't got no laces, is to tighten the foot, see? Walk about
with a tight foot, see? Well, that's no good for the foot. Puts
a bad strain on the foot. If you can do the shoes up proper
there's less chance of you getting a strain.

  ASTON *goes round to the top of his bed.*

ASTON. I might have some somewhere.

DAVIES. You see what I'm getting at?

  Pause.

ASTON. Here's some. (*He hands them to* DAVIES.)

DAVIES. These are brown.

ASTON. That's all I got.

DAVIES. These shoes are black.

  ASTON *does not answer.*

Well, they can do, anyway, until I get another pair.

  DAVIES *sits in the chair and begins to lace his shoes.*

Maybe they'll get me down to Sidcup tomorrow. If I get
down there I'll be able to sort myself out.

  Pause.

I've been offered a good job. Man has offered it to me, he's
... he's got plenty of ideas. He's got a bit of a future. But
they want my papers, you see, they want my references. I'd
have to get down to Sidcup before I could get hold of them.
That's where they are, see. Trouble is, getting there. That's
my problem. The weather's dead against it.

ASTON *quietly exits, unnoticed.*

Don't know as these shoes'll be much good. It's a hard road,
I been down there before. Coming the other way, like. Last
time I left there, it was ... last time ... getting on a
while back ... the road was bad, the rain was coming

down, lucky I didn't die there on the road, but I got here, I
kept going, all along . . . yes . . . I kept going all along.
But all the same, I can't go on like this, what I got to do, I
got to get back there, find this man—

He turns and looks about the room.

Christ! That bastard, he ain't even listening to me!

BLACKOUT.
DIM LIGHT THROUGH THE WINDOW.
It is night. ASTON *and* DAVIES *are in bed,* DAVIES *groaning.*
ASTON *sits up, gets out of bed, switches on the light, goes
over to* DAVIES *and shakes him.*

ASTON. Hey, stop it, will you? I can't sleep.

DAVIES. What? What? What's going on?

ASTON. You're making noises.

DAVIES. I'm an old man, what do you expect me to do, stop
breathing?

ASTON. You're making noises.

DAVIES. What do you expect me to do, stop breathing?

ASTON *goes to his bed, and puts on his trousers.*

ASTON. I'll get a bit of air.

DAVIES. What do you expect me to do? I tell you, mate, I'm
not surprised they took you in. Waking an old man up in the
middle of the night, you must be off your nut! Giving me
bad dreams, who's responsible, then, for me having bad
dreams? If you wouldn't keep mucking me about I wouldn't
make no noises! How do you expect me to sleep peaceful
when you keep poking me all the time? What do you want
me to do, stop breathing?

*He throws the cover off and gets out of bed, wearing his vest,
waistcoat and trousers.*

It's getting so freezing in here I have to keep my trousers on
to go to bed. I never done that before in my life. But that's

what I got to do here. Just because you won't put in any bleeding heating! I've had just about enough with you mucking me about. I've seen better days than you have, man. Nobody ever got me inside one of them places, anyway. I'm a sane man! So don't you start mucking me about. I'll be all right as long as you keep your place. Just you keep your place, that's all. Because I can tell you, your brother's got his eye on you. He knows all about you. I got a friend there, don't you worry about that. I got a true pal there. Treating me like dirt! Why'd you invite me in here in the first place if you was going to treat me like this? You think you're better than me you got another think coming. I know enough. They had you inside one of them places before, they can have you inside again. Your brother's got his eye on you! They can put the pincers on your head again, man! They can have them on again! Any time. All they got to do is get the word. They'd carry you in there, boy. They'd come here and pick you up and carry you in! They'd keep you fixed! They'd put them pincers on your head, they'd have you fixed! They'd take one look at all this junk I got to sleep with they'd know you were a creamer. That was the greatest mistake they made, you take my tip, letting you get out of that place. Nobody knows what you're at, you go out you come in, nobody knows what you're at! Well, nobody messes me about for long. You think I'm going to do your dirty work? Haaaaahhhhh! You better think again! You want me to do all the dirty work all up and down them stairs just so I can sleep in this lousy filthy hole every night? Not me, boy. Not for you boy. You don't know what you're doing half the time. You're up the creek! You're half off! You can tell it by looking at you. Who ever saw you slip me a few bob? Treating me like a bloody animal! I never been inside a nuthouse!

    ASTON *makes a slight move towards him.* DAVIES *takes his knife from his back pocket.*

Don't come nothing with me, mate. I got this here. I used
it. I used it. Don't come it with me.

    A pause. They stare at each other.

Mind what you do now.

    Pause.

Don't you try anything with me.

    Pause.

ASTON. I . . . I think it's about time you found somewhere
    else. I don't think we're hitting it off.

DAVIES. Find somewhere else?

ASTON. Yes.

DAVIES. Me? You talking to me? Not me, man! You!

ASTON. What?

DAVIES. You! You better find somewhere else!

ASTON. I live here. You don't.

DAVIES. Don't I? Well, I live here. I been offered a job here.

ASTON. Yes *:* . . well, I don't think you're really suitable.

DAVIES. Not suitable? Well, I can tell you, there's someone
    here thinks I am suitable. And I'll tell you. I'm staying on
    here as caretaker! Get it! Your brother, he's told me, see,
    he's told me the job is mine. Mine! So that's where I am.
    I'm going to be his caretaker.

ASTON. My brother?

DAVIES. He's staying, he's going to run this place, and I'm
    staying with him.

ASTON. Look. If I give you . . . a few bob you can get down
    to Sidcup.

DAVIES. You build your shed first! A few bob! When I can
    earn a steady wage here! You build your stinking shed first!
    That's what!

    ASTON *stares at him.*

ASTON. That's not a stinking shed.

    Silence.

    ASTON *moves to him.*

It's clean. It's all good wood. I'll get it up. No trouble.

DAVIES. Don't come too near!

ASTON. You've no reason to call that shed stinking.

DAVIES points the knife.

You stink.

DAVIES. What!

ASTON. You've been stinking the place out.

DAVIES. Christ, you say that to me!

ASTON. For days. That's one reason I can't sleep.

DAVIES. You call me that! You call me stinking!

ASTON. You better go.

DAVIES. I'LL STINK YOU!

He thrusts his arm out, the arm trembling, the knife pointing at ASTON'S *stomach.* ASTON *does not move. Silence.* DAVIES' *arm moves no further. They stand.*

I'll stink you. . . .

Pause.

ASTON. Get your stuff.

DAVIES draws the knife in to his chest, breathing heavily. ASTON *goes to* DAVIES' *bed, collects his bag and puts a few of* DAVIES' *things into it.*

DAVIES. You ain't . . . you ain't got the right . . . Leave that alone, that's mine!

DAVIES takes the bag and presses the contents down.

All right . . . I been offered a job here . . . you wait . . . (*He puts on his smoking-jacket.*) . . you wait . . . your brother . . . he'll sort you out . . . you call me that . . . you call me that . . . no one's ever called me that ·. . (*He puts on his overcoat.*) You'll be sorry you called me that . . . . you ain't heard the last of this . . . (*He picks up his bag and goes to the door.*) You'll be sorry you called me that. . . .

He opens the door, ASTON *watching him.*

Now I know who I can trust.

DAVIES *goes out.* ASTON *stands.*

BLACKOUT.

LIGHTS UP. *Early evening.*

Voices on the stairs.

MICK *and* DAVIES *enter.*

DAVIES. Stink! You hear that! Me! I told you what he said, didn't I? Stink! You hear that? That's what he said to me!

MICK. Tch, tch, tch.

DAVIES. That's what he said to me.

MICK. You don't stink.

DAVIES. No, sir!

MICK. If you stank I'd be the first one to tell you.

DAVIES. I told him, I told him he . . . I said to him, you ain't heard the last of this man! I said, don't you forget your brother. I told him you'd be coming along to sort him out. He don't know what he's started, doing that. Doing that to me. I said to him, I said to him, he'll be along, your brother'll be along, he's got sense, not like you—

MICK. What do you mean?

DAVIES. Eh?

MICK. You saying my brother hasn't got any sense?

DAVIES. What? What I'm saying is, you got ideas for this place, all this . . . all this decorating, see? I mean, he's got no right to order me about. I take orders from you, I do my caretaking for you, I mean, you look upon me . . . you don't treat me like a lump of dirt . . . we can both . . . we can both see him for what he is.

Pause.

MICK. What did he say then, when you told him I'd offered you the job as caretaker?

DAVIES. He . . . he said . . . he said . . . something about. . . he lived here.

MICK. Yes, he's got a point, en he?

DAVIES. A point! This is your house, en't? You let him live here!

MICK. I could tell him to go, I suppose.

DAVIES. That's what I'm saying.

MICK. Yes. I could tell him to go. I mean, I'm the landlord. On the other hand, he's the sitting tenant. Giving him notice, you see, what it is, it's a technical matter, that's what it is. It depends how you regard this room. I mean it depends whether you regard this room as furnished or un-furnished. See what I mean?

DAVIES. No, I don't.

MICK. All this furniture, you see, in here, it's all his, except the beds, of course. So what it is, it's a fine legal point, that's what it is.

Pause.

DAVIES. I tell you he should go back where he come from!

MICK (*turning to look at him*). Come from?

DAVIES. Yes.

MICK. Where did he come from?

DAVIES. Well . . . he . . . he. . . .

MICK. You get a bit out of your depth sometimes, don't you?
Pause.
(*Rising, briskly.*) Well, anyway, as things stand, I don't mind having a go at doing up the place. . . .

DAVIES. That's what I wanted to hear!

MICK. No, I don't mind.
He turns to face DAVIES.
But you better be as good as you say you are.

DAVIES. What do you mean?

MICK. Well, you say you're an interior decorator, you'd better be a good one.

DAVIES. A what?

MICK. What do you mean, a what? A decorator. An interior decorator.

DAVIES. Me? What do you mean? I never touched that. I never been that.

MICK. You've never what?

DAVIES. No, no, not me, man. I'm not an interior decorator. I been too busy. Too many other things to do, you see. But I . . . but I could always turn my hand to most things . . . give me . . . give me a bit of time to pick it up.

MICK. I don't want you to pick it up. I want a first-class experienced interior decorator. I thought you were one.

DAVIES. Me? Now wait a minute— wait a minute—you got the wrong man.

MICK. How could I have the wrong man? You're the only man I've spoken to. You're the only man I've told, about my dreams, about my deepest wishes, you're the only one I've told, and I only told you because I understood you were an experienced first-class professional interior and exterior decorator.

DAVIES. Now look here—

MICK. You mean you wouldn't know how to fit teal-blue, copper and parchment linoleum squares and have those colours re-echoed in the walls?

DAVIES. Now, look here, where'd you get—?

MICK. You wouldn't be able to decorate out a table in afro-mosia teak veneer, an armchair in oatmeal tweed and a beech frame settee with a woven sea-grass seat?

DAVIES. I never said that!

MICK. Christ! I must have been under a false impression!

DAVIES. I never said it!

MICK. You're a bloody impostor, mate!

DAVIES. Now you don't want to say that sort of thing to me. You took me on here as caretaker. I was going to give you a helping hand, that's all, for a small . . for a small wage, I never said nothing about that . . . you start calling me names—

MICK. What is your name?

DAVIES. Don't start that—

MICK. No, what's your real name?

DAVIES. My real name's Davies.

MICK. What's the name you go under?

DAVIES. Jenkins!

MICK. You got two names. What about the rest? Eh? Now come on, why did you tell me all this dirt about you being an interior decorator?

DAVIES. I didn't tell you nothing! Won't you listen to what I'm saying?

Pause.

It was him who told you. It was your brother who must have told you. He's nutty! He'd tell you anything, out of spite, he's nutty, he's half way gone, it was him who told you.

MICK *walks slowly to him.*

MICK. What did you call my brother?

DAVIES. When?

MICK. He's what?

DAVIES. I . . . now get this straight. . . .

MICK. Nutty? Who's nutty?

Pause.

Did you call my brother nutty? My brother. That's a bit of . . . . that's a bit of an impertinent thing to say, isn't it?

DAVIES. But he says so himself!

MICK *walks slowly round* DAVIES' *figure, regarding him, once. He circles him, once.*

MICK. What a strange man you are. Aren't you? You're really strange. Ever since you come into this house there's been nothing but trouble. Honest. I can take nothing you say at face value. Every word you speak is open to any number of different interpretations. Most of what you say is lies. You're violent, you're erratic, you're just completely unpredictable. You're nothing else but a wild animal, when you come down to it. You're a barbarian. And to put the old tin lid on it, you stink from arse-hole to breakfast time. Look at it. You come here recommending yourself as an interior decorator, where-upon I take you on, and what happens? You make a long speech about all the references you've got down at Sidcup, and what happens? I haven't noticed you go down to Sidcup to obtain them. It's all most regrettable but it looks as though I'm compelled to pay you off for your caretaking work. Here's half a dollar.

He feels in his pocket, takes out a half-crown and tosses it at DAVIES' *feet.* DAVIES *stands still.* MICK *walks to the gas stove and picks up the Buddha.*

DAVIES (*slowly*). All right then ... you do that ... you do it ... if that's what you want. ...

MICK. THAT'S WHAT I WANT!

He hurls the Buddha against the gas stove. It breaks.
(*Passionately.*) Anyone would think this house was all I got to worry about. I got plenty of other things I can worry about. I've got other things. I've got plenty of other interests. I've got my own business to build up, haven't I? I got to think about expanding ... in all directions. I don't stand still. I'm moving about, all the time. I'm moving ... all the time. I've got to think about the future. I'm not worried about this house. I'm not interested. My brother can worry about it. He can do it up, he can decorate it, he can do what he likes with it. I'm not bothered. I thought I was doing him a favour, letting him live here. He's got his own ideas. Let him have them. I'm going to chuck it in.

Pause.

DAVIES. What about me?

Silence. MICK *does not look at him.*
A door bangs.

Silence. They do not move.

ASTON *comes in. He closes the door, moves into the room and faces* MICK. *They look at each other. Both are smiling, faintly.*

MICK (*beginning to speak to* ASTON). Look. . . uh . . .
He stops, goes to the door and exits. ASTON *leaves the door open, crosses behind* DAVIES, *sees the broken Buddha, and looks at the pieces for a moment. He then goes to his bed, takes off his overcoat, sits, takes the screwdriver and plug and pokes the plug.*

DAVIES. I just come back for my pipe.

ASTON. Oh yes.

DAVIES. I got out and . . . half way down I . . . I suddenly . . . found out . . . you see . . . that I hadn't got my pipe. So I come back to get it. . . .
Pause. He moves to ASTON.
That ain't the same plug, is it, you been . . .?
Pause.
Still can't get anywhere with it, eh?
Pause.
Well, if you . . . persevere, in my opinion, you'll probably . . .
Pause.
Listen. . . .
Pause.
You didn't mean that, did you, about me stinking, did you?
Pause.
Did you? You been a good friend to me. You took me in. You took me in, you didn't ask me no questions, you give me a bed, you been a mate to me. Listen. I been thinking, why I made all them noises, it was because of the draught, see, that draught was on me as I was sleeping, made me make noises without me knowing it, so I been thinking, what I mean to say, if you was to give me your bed, and you have

my bed, there's not all that difference between them, they're the same sort of bed, if I was to have yourn, you sleep, wherever bed you're in, so you have mine, I have yourn, and that'll be all right, I'll be out of the draught, see, I mean, you don't mind a bit of wind, you need a bit of air, I can understand that, you being in that place that time, with all them doctors and all they done, closed up, I know them places, too hot, you see, they're always too hot, I had a peep in one once, nearly suffocated me, so I reckon that'd be the best way out of it, we swap beds, and then we could get down to what we was saying, I'd look after the place for you, I'd keep an eye on it for you, for you, like, not for the other . . . not for . . . for your brother, you see, not for him, for you, I'll be your man, you say the word, just say the word. . . .

    Pause.

What do you think of this I'm saying?

    Pause.

ASTON. No, I like sleeping in this bed.

DAVIES. But you don't understand my meaning!

ASTON. Anyway, that one's my brother's bed.

DAVIES. Your brother?

ASTON. Any time he stays here. This is my bed. It's the only bed I can sleep in.

DAVIES. But your brother's gone! He's gone!

    Pause.

ASTON. No. I couldn't change beds.

DAVIES. But you don't understand my meaning!

ASTON. Anyway, I'm going to be busy. I've got that shed to get up. If I don't get it up now it'll never go up. Until it's up I can't get started.

DAVIES. I'll give you a hand to put up your shed, that's what I'll do!

    Pause.

I'll give you a hand! We'll both put up that shed together!
See? Get it done in next to no time! Do you see what
I'm saying?

Pause.

ASTON. No. I can get it up myself.
DAVIES. But listen. I'm with you, I'll be here, I'll do it for
you!

Pause.

We'll do it together!

Pause.

Christ, we'll change beds!

ASTON *moves to the window and stands with his back to*
DAVIES.

You mean you're throwing me out? You can't do that.
Listen man, listen man, I don't mind, you see, I don't mind,
I'll stay, I don't mind, I'll tell you what, if you don't want
to change beds, we'll keep it as it is, I'll stay in the same bed,
maybe if I can get a stronger piece of sacking, like, to go
over the window, keep out the draught, that'll do it, what do
you say, we'll keep it as it is?

Pause.

ASTON. No.
DAVIES. Why . . . not?

ASTON *turns to look at him.*

ASTON. You make too much noise.
DAVIES. But . . . but . . . look . . . listen . . . listen here . . .
I mean. . . .

ASTON *turns back to the window.*

What am I going to do?

Pause.

What shall I do?

Pause.

Where am I going to go?

Pause.

If you want me to go . . . I'll go. You just say the word.

Pause.

I'll tell you what though . . . them shoes . . . them shoes you give me . . . they're working out all right . . . they're all right. Maybe I could . . . get down. . . .

ASTON *remains still, his back to him, at the window.*

Listen . . . if I . . . got down . . . if I was to . . . get my papers . . . would you . . . would you let . . . would you . . . if I got down . . . and got my. . . .

Long silence.

Curtain.

The Dwarfs

The Dwarfs was first performed on the B.B.C. Third Programme on 2 December, 1960 with the following cast:-

LEN   Richard Pasco
PETE   Jon Rollason
MARK   Alex Scott

Produced by Barbara Bray

The play was first presented in a new version for the stage by Michael Codron and David Hall at the New Arts Theatre, London, on 18 September, 1963 with the following cast:-

LEN   John Hurt
PETE   Philip Bond
MARK   Michael Forrest

Directed by Harold Pinter
assisted by Guy Vaesen

The Dwarfs

The two main areas are:

1. a room in LEN'S *house. Solid middle-European furniture. Piles of books. A small carved table with a chenille cloth, a bowl of fruit, books. Two marquetry chairs. A hanging lamp with dark shade.*

2. the living room in MARK'S *flat. Quite modern. Comfortable. Two armchairs and a coffee table.*

There is also a central downstage area of isolation and, for a short scene later in the play, a bed in a hospital, upstage on a higher level.

LEN, PETE *and* MARK *are all in their late twenties.*

MARK'S *room, midnight. Lamps are alight. Two cups and saucers, a sugar-bowl and a teapot are on a tray on the coffee table.*

PETE *is sitting, reading.*

LEN *is playing a recorder. The sound is fragmentary.*

LEN: Pete.
PETE: What?
LEN: Come here.
PETE: What?
LEN: What's the matter with this recorder? [*He pulls recorder in half, looks down, blows, taps.*] There's something wrong with this recorder.
PETE: Let's have some tea.

LEN: I can't do a thing with it.

[*Re-assembles recorder. Another attempt to play.*]

Where's the milk?

[*He puts recorder on tray.*]

PETE: You were going to bring it.

LEN: That's right.

PETE: Well, where is it?

LEN: I forgot it. Why didn't you remind me?

PETE: Give me the cup.

LEN: What do we do now?

PETE: Give me the tea.

LEN: Without milk?

PETE: There isn't any milk.

LEN: What about sugar? [*Moving towards door.*] He must have a pint of milk somewhere. [*He exits to kitchen. Noise of opening cupboards etc. He reappears with a couple of gherkins in a jar.*] Here's a couple of gherkins. What about a gherkin? [*Takes jar to* PETE.] Fancy a gherkin. [PETE *sniffs, looks up in disgust.* LEN *sniffs and exits.*] Wait a minute. [*Kitchen noises.* LEN *reappears with a bottle of milk.*] Ah! Here we are. I knew he'd have a pint laid on. [*Pressing the top.*] Uuh! Uuuhh .... It's stiff.

PETE: I wouldn't open that.

LEN: Uuuhh .... why not? I can't drink tea without milk. Uuh! That's it. [*Picking up cup to pour.*] Give us your cup.

PETE: Leave it alone.

[*Pause.* LEN *shakes bottle over cup.*]

LEN: It won't come out. [*Pause.*] The milk won't come out of the bottle.

PETE: It's been in there two weeks, why should it come out?

LEN: Two weeks? He's been away longer than two weeks. [*Slight pause.*] It's stuck in the bottle. [*Slight pause.*] You'd think a man like him would have a maid, wouldn't you, to look after the place while he's away, to look after his milk? Or a gentleman. A gentleman's gentleman. Are you quite sure he hasn't got a gentleman's gentleman tucked away somewhere, to look after the place for him?

PETE [*rising to replace book on shelf*]: Only you. You're the only gentleman's gentleman he's got.

[*Pause.*]

LEN: Well, if I'm his gentleman's gentleman, I should have been looking after the place for him.

[*Pause.* PETE *takes brass toasting fork off wall.*]

PETE: What's this?
LEN: That? You've seen that before. It's a toasting fork.
PETE: It's got a monkey's head.
LEN: It's Portuguese. Everything in this house is Portuguese.
PETE: Why's that?
LEN: That's where he comes from.
PETE: Does he?
LEN: Or at least, his grandmother on his father's side. That's where the family comes from.
PETE: Well, well.

[*He hangs up the toasting fork.*]

LEN: What time's he coming?
PETE: Soon.

[*He pours himself a cup of tea.*]

LEN: You're drinking black tea.
PETE: What about it?
LEN: You're not in Poland.

[*He plays recorder.* PETE *sits in armchair.*]

PETE: What's the matter with that thing?
LEN: Nothing. There's nothing wrong with it. But it must be

broken. It's a year since I played it. [*He sneezes.*] Aah! I've got the most shocking blasted cold I've ever had in all my life. [*He blows his nose.*] Still, it's not much of a nuisance really.

PETE: Don't wear me out. [*Slight pause.*] Why don't you pull yourself together? You'll be ready for the loony bin next week if you go on like this.

[LEN *uses recorder as a telescope to the back of* PETE'S *head.*]

[*Pause.*]

LEN: Ten to one he'll be hungry.

PETE: Who?

LEN: Mark. When he comes. He can eat like a bullock, that bloke. Still, he won't find much to come home to, will he? There's nothing in the kitchen, there's not even a bit of lettuce. It's like the workhouse here. [*Pause.*] He can eat like a bullock, that bloke. [*Pause.*] I've seen him finish off a loaf of bread before I'd got my jacket off. [*Pause.*] He'd never leave a breadcrumb on a plate in the old days. [*Pause.*] Of course, he may have changed. Things do change. But I'm the same. Do you know, I had five solid square meals one day last week? At eleven o'clock, two o'clock, six o'clock, ten o'clock and one o'clock. Not bad going. Work makes me hungry. I was working that day. [*Pause.*] I'm always starving when I get up. Daylight has a funny effect on me. As for the night, that goes without saying. As far as I'm concerned the only thing you can do in the night is eat. It keeps me fit, especially if I'm at home. I have to run downstairs to put the kettle on, run upstairs to finish what I'm doing, run downstairs to cut a sandwich or arrange a salad, run upstairs to finish what I'm doing, run back downstairs to see to the sausages, if I'm having sausages, run back upstairs to finish what I'm doing, run back downstairs to lay the table, run back upstairs to finish what I'm doing, run back—

PETE: Yes!

LEN: Where did you get those shoes?

PETE: What?

LEN: Those shoes. How long have you had them?

PETE: What's the matter with them?

LEN: Have you been wearing them all night?

[*Pause.*]

PETE: When did you last sleep?

[*His hand is lying open, palm upward.*]

LEN: Sleep? Don't make me laugh. All I do is sleep.

PETE: What about work? How's work?

LEN: Paddington? It's a big railway station. An oven. It's an
oven. Still, bad air is better than no air. It's best on night
shift. The trains come in, I give a bloke half a dollar, he
does my job, I curl up in the corner and read the timetables.
But they tell me I might make a first class porter. I've been
told I've got the makings of a number one porter. What are
you doing with your hand?

PETE: What are you talking about?

LEN: What are you doing with your hand?

PETE [*coolly*]: What do you think I'm doing with it? Eh?
What do you think?

LEN: I don't know.

PETE: I'll tell you, shall I? Nothing. I'm not doing anything
with it. It's not moving. I'm doing *nothing* with it.

LEN: You're holding it palm upwards.

PETE: What about it?

LEN: It's not normal. Let's have a look at that hand. Let's have
a look at it. [*Pause. He gasps through his teeth.*] You're a
homicidal maniac.

PETE: Is that a fact?

LEN: Look. Look at that hand. Look, look at it. A straight line right across the middle. Right across the middle, see? Horizontal. That's all you've got. What else have you got? You're a nut.

PETE: Oh yes?

LEN: You couldn't find two men in a million with a hand like that. It sticks out a mile. A mile. That's what you are, that's exactly what you are, you're a homicidal maniac!

[*A knock on the outer door.*]

PETE [*rising to exit*]: That's him. [*He goes off. The lights begin to fade to blackout.*]

MARK: [*off*] Anyone here?

PETE: [*off*] Yes, how are you?

MARK: [*off*] Any tea?

PETE: [*off*] Polish tea.

[*Blackout. The lights come up in* LEN'S *room—overhead lamp.*

LEN *is sitting at the side of the table.*]

LEN: There is my table. That is a table. There is my chair. There is my table. That is a bowl of fruit. There is my chair. There are my curtains. There is no wind. It is past night and before morning. This is my room. This is a room. There is the wall-paper, on the walls. There are six walls. Eight walls. An octagon. This room is an octagon.

There are my shoes, on my feet.

This is a journey and an ambush. This is the centre of the cold, a halt to the journey and no ambush. This is the deep grass I keep to. This is the thicket in the centre of the night and the morning. There is my hundred watt bulb like a dagger. This room moves. This room is moving. It has moved. It has reached . . . a dead halt. This is my fixture. There is no web. All's clear, and abundant. Perhaps a morning will arrive. If a morning arrives, it will not destroy my fixture, nor my luxury. If it is dark in the night or light,

nothing obtrudes. I have my compartment. I am wedged.
Here is my arrangement, and my kingdom. There are no
voices. They make no hole in my side.

The doorbell rings. LEN *searches for his glasses on the table,*
rummaging among the books. Lifts tablecloth. Is still. Searches
in armchair. Then on mantlepiece. Bell rings again. He
searches under table. Bell rings again. He rises, looks down,
sees glasses in top pocket of jacket. Smiles, puts them on.
Exits to open front door. MARK *enters to below table.* LEN
follows.

LEN: What's this, a suit? Where's your carnation?

MARK: What do you think of it?

LEN: It's not a schmutta.

MARK: It's got a zip at the hips.

LEN: A zip at the hips? What for?

MARK: Instead of a buckle. It's neat.

LEN: Neat? I should say it's neat.

MARK: No turn-ups.

LEN: I can see that. Why didn't you have turn-ups?

MARK: It's smarter without turn-ups.

LEN: Of course it's smarter without turn-ups.

MARK: I didn't want it double-breasted.

LEN: Double-breasted? Of course you couldn't have it double-
breasted.

MARK: What do you think of the cloth?

LEN: The cloth? [*He examines it, gasps and whistles through his*
teeth. At a great pace.] What a piece of cloth. What a piece
of cloth. What a piece of cloth. What a piece of cloth.
What a piece of *cloth.*

MARK: You like the cloth?

LEN: WHAT A PIECE OF CLOTH!

MARK: What do you think of the cut?

LEN: What do I think of the cut? The cut? The cut? What a cut!

What a cut! I've never seen such a cut! [*Pause.*] [*He sits and groans.*]

MARK [*combing his hair and sitting*]: Do you know where I've just been?

LEN: Where?

MARK: Earls Court.

LEN: Uuuuhh! What were you doing there? That's beside the point.

MARK: What's the matter with Earl's Court?

LEN: It's a mortuary without a corpse. [*Pause.*] There's a time and place for everything . . .

MARK: You're right there.

LEN: What do you mean by that?

MARK: There's a time and place for everything.

LEN: You're right there. [*Puts glasses on, rises to Mark.*] Who have you been with? Actors and actresses? What's it like when you act? Does it please you? Does it please anyone else?

MARK: What's wrong with acting?

LEN: It's a time-honoured profession—it's time-honoured. [*Pause.*] But what does it do? Does it please you when you walk onto a stage and everybody looks up and watches you? Maybe they don't want to watch you at all. Maybe they'd prefer to watch someone else. Have you ever asked them? [MARK *chuckles.*] You should follow my example and take up mathematics. [*Showing him open book.*] Look! All last night I was working at mechanics and determinants. There's nothing like a bit of calculus to cheer you up.

Pause.

MARK: I'll think about it.

LEN: Have you got a telephone here?

MARK: It's your house.

LEN: Yes. What are you doing here? What do you want here?

MARK: I thought you might give me some bread and honey.

LEN: I don't want you to become too curious in this room. There's no place for curiosities here. Keep a sense of proportion. That's all I ask.

MARK: That's all.

LEN: I've got enough on my plate with this room as it is.

MARK: What's the matter with it?

LEN: The rooms we live in . . . open and shut. [*Pause.*] Can't you see? They change shape at their own will. I wouldn't grumble if only they would keep to some consistency. But they don't. And I can't tell the limits, the boundaries, which I've been led to believe are natural. I'm all for the natural behaviour of rooms, doors, staircases, the lot. But I can't rely on them. When, for example, I look through a train window, at night, and see the yellow lights, very clearly, I can see what they are, and I see that they're still. But they're only still because I'm moving. I know that they do move along with me, and when we go round a bend, they bump off. But I know that they are still, just the same. They are, after all, stuck on poles which are rooted to the earth. So they must be still, in their own right, insofar as the earth itself is still, which of course it isn't. The point is, in a nutshell, that I can only appreciate such facts when I'm moving. When I'm still, nothing around me follows a natural course of conduct. I'm not saying I'm any criterion, I wouldn't say that. After all, when I'm on the train I'm not really moving at all. That's obvious. I'm in the corner seat. I'm still. I am perhaps being moved, but I do not move. Neither do the yellow lights. The train moves, granted, but what's a train got to do with it?

MARK: Nothing.

LEN: You're frightened.

MARK: Am I?

LEN: You're frightened that any moment I'm liable to put a red
hot burning coal in your mouth.

MARK: Am I?

LEN: But when the time comes, you see, what I shall do is place
the red hot burning coal in my own mouth.

Swift blackout. PETE *sits where* MARK *has been. Lights snap
up.*

I've got some beigels.

PETE: This is a very solid table, isn't it?

LEN: I said I've got some biegels.

PETE: No thanks. How long have you had this table?

LEN: It's a family heirloom.

PETE: Yes, I'd like a good table, and a good chair. Solid stuff.
Made for the bearer. I'd put them in a boat. Sail it down
the river. A houseboat. You could sit in the cabin and look
out at the water.

LEN: Who'd be steering?

PETE: You could park it. Park it. There's not a soul in sight.

LEN *brings half-full bottle of wine and glass to table. Reads
label. Sniffs at bottle. Pours some into glass, savours then
gargles, walking about. Spits wine back into glass, returns
bottle and glass at sideboard, after a defensive glance at* PETE.
Returns to above table.

LEN [*muttering*]: Impossible, impossible, impossible.

PETE [*briskly*]: I've been thinking about you.

LEN: Oh?

PETE: Do you know what your trouble is? You're not elastic.
There's no elasticity in you. You want to be more elastic.

LEN: Elastic? Elastic. Yes, you're quite right. Elastic. What are
you talking about?

PETE: Giving up the ghost isn't so much a failure as a tactical
error. By elastic I mean being prepared for your own

deviations. You don't know where you're going to come out next at the moment. You're like a rotten old shirt. Buck your ideas up. They'll lock you up before you're much older.

LEN: No. There is a different sky each time I look. The clouds run about in my eye. I can't do it.

PETE: The apprehension of experience must obviously be dependent upon discrimination if it's to be considered valuable. That's what you lack. You've got no idea how to preserve a distance between what you smell and what you think about it. You haven't got the faculty for making a simple distinction between one thing and another. Every time you walk out of this door you go straight over a cliff. What you've got to do is nourish the power of assessment. How can you hope to assess and verify anything if you walk about with your nose stuck between your feet all day long? You knock around with Mark too much. He can't do you any good. I know how to handle him. But I don't think he's your sort. Between you and me, I sometimes think he's a man of weeds. Sometimes I think he's just playing a game. But what game? I like him all right when you come down to it. We're old pals. But you look at him and what do you see? An attitude. Has it substance or is it barren? Sometimes I think it's as barren as a bombed site. He'll be a spent force in no time if he doesn't watch his step. [*Pause.*] I'll tell you a dream I had last night. I was with a girl in a tube station, on the platform. People were rushing about. There was some sort of panic. When I looked round I saw everyone's faces were peeling, blotched, blistered. People were screaming, booming down the tunnels. There was a fire bell clanging. When I looked at the girl I saw that her face was coming off in slabs too, like plaster. Black scabs and stains. The skin was dropping off like lumps of cat's meat. I could hear it sizzling on the electric rails. I pulled her by the arm to get her out of there.

She wouldn't budge. Stood there, with half a face, staring at me. I screamed at her to come away. Then I thought, Christ, what's my face like? Is that why she's staring? Is that rotting too?

Lights change. LEN'S *room.* PETE *and* MARK *looking at chess board.* LEN *watching them. Silence.*

LEN: Eh . . .

[*They don't look up.*]

The dwarfs are back on the job. [*Pause.*] I said the dwarfs are back on the job.

MARK: The what?

LEN: The dwarfs.

MARK: Oh yes?

LEN: Oh yes. They've been waiting for a smoke signal you see. I've just sent up the smoke signal.

[*Pause.*]

MARK: You've just sent it up, have you?

LEN: Yes. I've called them in on the job. They've taken up their positions. Haven't you noticed?

PETE: I haven't noticed. [*To* MARK.] Have you noticed?

MARK *chuckles.*

LEN: But I'll tell you one thing. They don't stop work until the job in hand is finished, one way or another. They never run out on a job. Oh no. They're true professionals. Real professionals.

PETE: Listen. Can't you see we're trying to play chess?

Pause.

LEN: I've called them in to keep an eye on you two, you see. They're going to keep a very close eye on you. So am I. We're waiting for you to show your hand. We're all going to keep a very close eye on you two. Me and the dwarfs.

Pause.

MARK: [*referring to chess*]: I think I've got you knackered, Pete.

PETE *looks at him.*

PETE: Do you?

Lights change and come up full in MARK'S *room.* LEN *enters with old gilt mirror.* MARK *follows.*

MARK: Put that mirror back.

LEN: This is the best piece of furniture you've got in the house. It's Spanish. No Portuguese. You're Portuguese, aren't you?

MARK: Put it back.

LEN: Look at your face in this mirror. Look. It's a farce. Where are your features? You haven't got any features. You couldn't call those features. What are you going to do about it, eh? What's the answer?

MARK: Mind that mirror. It's not insured.

LEN: I saw Pete the other day. In the evening. You didn't know that. I wonder about you. I often wonder about you. But I must keep pedalling. I must. There's a time limit. Who have you got hiding here? You're not alone here. What about your Esperanto? Don't forget, anything over two ounces goes up a penny.

MARK: Thanks for the tip.

LEN: Here's your mirror.

MARK exits with mirror. LEN *picks out apple from a fruit bowl, sits in armchair staring at it.* MARK *returns.*

This is a funny-looking apple.

[*He tosses it back to* MARK, *who replaces it.*]

Pete asked me to lend him a shilling.

MARK: Uh?

LEN: I refused.

MARK: What?

LEN: I refused downright to lend him a shilling.

MARK: What did he say to that?

LEN: Plenty. Since I left him I've been thinking thoughts I've never thought before. I've been. thinking thoughts I've never thought before.

MARK: You spend too much time with Pete.

LEN: What?

MARK: Give it a rest. He doesn't do you any good. I'm the only one who knows how to get on with him. I can handle him. You can't. You take him too seriously. He doesn't worry me. I know how to handle him. He doesn't take any liberties with me.

LEN: Who says he takes liberties with me? Nobody takes liberties with me. I'm not the sort of man you can take liberties with.

MARK: You should drop it.

LEN *sees toasting fork, takes it to* MARK.

LEN: This is a funny toasting fork. Do you ever make any toast?

He drops the fork on the floor.

Don't touch it! You don't know what will happen if you touch it! You mustn't touch it! You mustn't bend! Wait. [*Pause.*] I'll bend. I'll . . . pick it up. I'm going to touch it. [*Pause . . . softly.*] There. You see? Nothing happens when I touch it. Nothing. Nothing can happen. No one would bother. [*A broken sigh.*] You see, I can't see the broken glass. I can't see the mirror I have to look through. I see the other side. The other side. But I can't see the mirror side. [*Pause.*] I want to break it, all of it. But how can I break it? How can I break it when I can't see it?

Lights fade and come up again in MARK'S *room.* LEN *is sitting in an arm chair.* MARK *enters with whisky bottle and two glasses. He pours drinks for* PETE *and himself.* PETE, *who has followed him in, takes his glass.* MARK *sits in other armchair. Neither take any notice of* LEN.

Silence.

PETE: Thinking got me into this and thinking's got to get me out. You know what I want? An efficient idea. You know what I mean? An efficient idea. One that'll work. Something I can pin my money on. An each way bet. Nothing's guaranteed, I know that. But I'm willing to gamble. I gambled when I went to work in the city. I want to fight them on their own ground, not moan about them from a distance. I did it and I'm still living. But I've had my fill of these city guttersnipes—all that scavenging scum! They're the sort of people, who, if the gates of heaven opened to them, all they'd feel would be a draught. I'm wasting away down there. The time has come to act. I'm after something truly workable, something deserving of the proper and active and voluntary application of my own powers. And I'll find it.

LEN: I squashed a tiny insect on a plate the other day. And I brushed the remains off my finger with my thumb. Then I saw that the fragments were growing, like fluff. As they were falling, they were becoming larger, like fluff. I had put my hand into the body of a dead bird.

PETE: The trouble is, you've got to be quite sure of what you mean by efficient. Look at a nutcracker. You press the cracker and the cracker cracks the nut. You might think that's an exact process. It's not. The nut cracks, but the hinge of the cracker gives out a friction which is completely incidental to the particular idea. It's unnecessary, an escape and wastage of energy to no purpose. So there's nothing efficient about a nutcracker. [*Pete sits, drinks*].

LEN: They've gone on a picnic.

MARK: Who?

LEN: The dwarfs.

PETE: Oh Christ. [*Picks up paper.*]

LEN: They've left me to sweep the yard, to keep the place in order. It's a bloody liberty. They're supposed to be keeping you under observation. What do they think I am, a bloody charlady? I can't look after the place by myself, it's not possible. Piles and piles and piles of muck and leavings all over the place, spewed up spewed up, I'm not a skivvy, they don't pay me, I pay them.

MARK: Why don't you settle down?

LEN: Oh don't worry, it's basically a happy relationship. I trust them. They're very efficient. They know what they're waiting for. But they've got a new game, did I tell you? It's to do with beetles and twigs. There's a rockery of red-hot cinder. I like watching them. Their hairs are curled and oily on their necks. Always squatting and bending, dipping their wicks in the custard. Now and again a lick of flame screws up their noses. Do you know what they do? They run wild. They yowl, they pinch, they dribble, they whimper, they gouge, and then they soothe each others' orifices with a local ointment, and then, all gone, all forgotten, they lark about, each with his buddy, get out the nose spray and the scented syringe, settle down for the night with a bun and a doughnut.

PETE: See you Mark. [*Exit.*]

MARK: Why don't you put it on the table? [*Pause.*] Open it up, Len. [*Pause.*] I'm supposed to be a friend of yours.

LEN: You're a snake in my house.

MARK: Really?

LEN: You're trying to buy and sell me. You think I'm a ventriloquist's dummy. You've got me pinned to the wall before I open my mouth. You've got a tab on me, you're buying me out of house and home, you're a calculating bastard. [*Pause.*] Answer me. Say something. [*Pause.*] Do you understand? [*Pause.*] You don't agree? [*Pause.*] You disagree? [*Pause.*] You think I'm mistaken? [*Pause.*] But am I? [*Pause.*] Both of you bastards, you've made a hole in my side, I can't plug it! [*Pause.*] I've lost a kingdom. I suppose you're taking good care of things. Did you know that you and Pete are a music hall act? What happens? What do you do when you're alone? Do you do a jig? I suppose you're taking good care of things. I've got my treasure too. It's in my corner. Everything's in my corner. Everything is from the corner's point of view. I don't hold the whip. I'm a labouring man. I do the corner's will. I slave my guts out. I thought, at one time, that I'd escaped it, but it never dies, it's never dead. I feed it, it's well fed. Things that at one time seem to me of value I have no resource but to give it to eat and what was of value turns into pus. I can hide nothing. I can't lay anything aside. Nothing can be put aside, nothing can be hidden, nothing can be saved, it waits, it eats, it's voracious, you're in it, Pete's in it, you're all in my corner. There must be somewhere else!

Swift cross fade of lights to down centre area.

PETE *is seen vaguely, standing downstage below* LEN'S *room.* MARK *is seated in his room. Unlit.* LEN *crouches, watching* PETE.

Pete walks by the river. Under the woodyard wall stops. Stops. Hiss of the yellow grass. The wood battlements jaw over the wall. Dust in the fairground ticks. The night ticks.

He hears the tick of the roundabout, up river with the sweat. Pete walks by the river. Under the woodyard wall stops. Stops. The wood hangs. Deathmask on the water. Pete walks by the — gull. Slicing gull. Gull. Down. He stops. Rat corpse in the yellow grass. Gull pads. Gull probes. Gull stamps his feet. Gull whinnies 'up. Gull screams, tears, Pete, tears, digs, Pete cuts, breaks, Pete stretches the corpse, flaps his wings, Pete's beak grows, probes, digs, pulls, the river jolts, no moon, what can I see, the dwarfs collect, they slide down the bridge, they scutter by the shoreside, the dwarfs collect, capable, industrious, they wear raincoats, it is going to rain, Pete digs, he screws in to the head, the dwarfs watch, Pete tugs, he tugs, he's tugging, he kills, he's killing, the rat's head, with a snap the cloth of the rat's head tears. Pete walks by the . . . [*Deep groan.*]

He sinks into chair left of his table. Lights in LEN'S *room swiftly fade up.* PETE *turns to him.*

PETE: You look the worse for wear. What's the matter with you?

LEN: I've been ill.

PETE: Ill? What's the matter?

LEN: Cheese. Stale cheese. It got me in the end. I've been eating a lot of cheese.

PETE: Yes, well, it's easy to eat too much cheese.

LEN: It all came out, in about twenty-eight goes. I couldn't stop shivering and I couldn't stop squatting. It got me all right. I'm all right now. I only go three times a day now. I can more or less regulate it. Once in the morning. A quick dash before lunch. Another quick dash after tea, and then I'm free to do what I want. I don't think you understand. That cheese didn't die. It only began to live when you swallowed it, you see, after it had gone down. I bumped into a German one night, he came home with me and helped me finish it off. He took it to bed with him, he sat up in bed with it, in the guest's suite. I went in and had a gander. He had it taped. He was brutal with it. He would bite into it and then concentrate. I had to hand it to him. The sweat came out on his nose but he stayed on his feet. After he'd got out of bed, that was. Stood bolt upright, swallowed it, clicked his fingers, ordered another piece of blackcurrant pie. It's my pie-making season. His piss stank worse than the cheese. You look in the pink.

PETE: You want to watch your step. You know that? You're going from bad to worse. Why don't you pull yourself together? Eh? Get a steady job. Cultivate a bit of go and guts for a change. Make yourself useful, mate, for Christ's sake. As you are, you're just a dead weight round everybody's neck. You want to listen to your friends, mate. Who else have you got?

PETE *taps him on the shoulder and exits. A light comes up on* MARK. *The lights in* LEN'S *room fade out.* LEN *rises to down centre.*

LEN: Mark sits by the fireside. Crosses his legs. His fingers wear a ring. The finger poised. Mark regards his finger. He regards his legs. He regards the fireside. Outside the door is the black blossom. He combs his hair with an ebony comb, he sits, he lies, he lowers his eyelashes, raises them, sees no change in the posture of the room, lights a cigarette, watches his hand clasp the lighter, watches the flame, sees his mouth go forward, sees the consummation, is satisfied. Pleased, sees the smoke in the lamp, pleased with the lamp and the smoke and his bulk, pleased with his legs and his ring and his hand and his body in the lamp. Sees himself speaking, the words arranged on his lips, sees himself with pleasure silent.

Under the twigs they slide, by the lilac bush, break the

stems, sit, scutter to the edge of the lawn and there wait, capable, industrious, put up their sunshades, watch. Mark lies, heavy, content, watches his smoke in the window, times his puff out, his hand fall, [*with growing disgust*] smiles at absent guests, sucks in all comers, arranges his web, lies there a spider.

LEN *moves to above armchair in* MARK'S *room as lights fade up. Down centre area fades out.*

What did you say?

MARK: I never said anything.

LEN: What do you do when you're tired, go to bed?

MARK: That's right.

LEN: You sleep like a log.

MARK: Yes.

LEN: What do you do when you wake up?

MARK: Wake up.

LEN: I want to ask you a question.

MARK: No doubt.

LEN: Are you prepared to answer questions?

MARK: No.

LEN: What do you do in the day when you're not walking about?

MARK: I rest.

LEN: Where do you find a resting place?

MARK: Here and there.

LEN: By consent?

MARK: Invariably.

LEN: But you're not particular?

MARK: Yes, I'm particular.

LEN: You choose your resting place?

MARK: Normally.

LEN: That might be anywhere?

MARK: Yes.

LEN: Does that content you?

MARK: Sure! I've got a home. I know where I live.

LEN: You mean you've got roots. Why haven't I got roots? My house is older than yours. My family lived here. Why haven't I got a home?

MARK: Move out.

LEN: Do you believe in God?

MARK: What?

LEN: Do you believe in God?

MARK: Who?

LEN: God.

MARK: God?

LEN: Do you believe in God?

MARK: Do I believe in God?

LEN: Yes.

MARK: Would you say that again?

LEN *goes swiftly to shelf. Picks up biscuit jar. Offers to* MARK.

LEN: Have a biscuit.

MARK: Thanks.

LEN: They're your biscuits.

MARK: There's two left. Have one yourself.

LEN *puts biscuits away.*

LEN: You don't understand. You'll never understand.

MARK: Really?

LEN: Do you know what the point is? Do you know what it is?

MARK: No.

LEN: The point is, who are you? Not why or how, not even what. I can see what, perhaps, clearly enough. But who are you? It's no use saying you know who you are just because you tell me you can fit your particular key into a particular slot, which will only receive your particular key because that's not foolproof and certainly not conclusive. Just because you're inclined to make these statements of faith has nothing to do with me. It's not my business. Occasionally I believe I perceive a little of what you are but that's pure accident. Pure accident on both our parts, the perceived and the perceiver. It's nothing like an accident, it's deliberate, it's a joint pretence. We depend on these accidents, on these contrived accidents, to continue. It's not important then that it's conspiracy or hallucination. What you are, or appear to be to me, or appear to be to you, changes so quickly, so horrifyingly, I certainly can't keep up with it and I'm damn sure you can't either. But who you are I can't even begin to recognize, and sometimes I recognize it so wholly, so forcibly, I can't look, and how can I be certain of what I see? You have no number. Where am I to look, where am I to look, what is there to locate, so as to have sòme surety, to have some rest from this whole bloody racket? You're the sum of so many reflections. How many reflections? Whose reflections? Is that what you consist of? What scum does the tide leave? What happens to the scum? When does it happen? I've seen what happens. But I can't speak when I see it. I can only point a finger. I can't even do that. The scum is broken and sucked back. I don't see where it goes. I don't see when, what do I see, what have I seen? What have I seen, the scum or the essence? What about it? Does all this give you the right to stand there and tell me you know who you are? It's a bloody impertinence. There's a great desert and there's a wind stopping. Pete's been eating too much cheese, he's ill from it, it's eating his flesh away, but that doesn't matter, you're still both in the same boat, you're eating all my biscuits, but that doesn't matter, you're still both in the same boat, you're still standing behind the curtains together. He thinks you're a fool, Pete thinks you're a fool, but that doesn't matter, you're still both of you standing behind my curtains, moving my curtains in my room. He may be your

Black Knight, you may be his Black Knight, but I'm cursed with the two of you, with two Black Knight's, that's friendship, that's this that I know. That's what I know.

MARK: Pete thinks I'm a fool? [*Pause.*] Pete . . . . Pete thinks that I'm a *fool*?

LEN *exits. Lights in* MARK'S *room fade out and then fade in again. Doorbell rings.* MARK *rises, goes off to front door.*

Silence.

PETE [*entering*]: Hullo, Mark.
MARK [*re-enters and sits again*]: Hullo.
PETE: What are you doing?
MARK: Nothing.
PETE: Can I sit down?
MARK: Sure.

Pete sits right armchair. Pause.

PETE: Well, what are you doing with yourself?
MARK: When's that?
PETE: Now.
MARK: Nothing.

MARK *files his nails.*

[*Pause.*]

PETE: Len's in hospital.
MARK: Len? What's the matter with him?
PETE: Kidney trouble. Not serious. [*Pause.*] Well, what have you been doing with yourself?
MARK: When?
PETE: Since I saw you.
MARK: This and that.
PETE: This and what?

MARK: That.

[*Pause.*]

PETE: Do you want to go and see Len?
MARK: When? Now?
PETE: Yes. It's visiting time. [*Pause.*] Are you busy?
MARK: No.

[*Pause.*]

PETE: What's up?
MARK: What?
PETE: What's up?
MARK: What do you mean?
PETE: You're wearing a gasmask.
MARK: Not me.

[*Pause.*]

PETE [*rising*]: Ready?
MARK: Yes. [*He rises and exits.*]
PETE [*as he follows* MARK *off*]: Fine day. [*Pause.*] Bit chilly.

The door slams as they leave the house. Lights up on LEN *in
hospital bed. Listening to wireless (earphones).*

PETE *and* MARK *enter.*

LEN: You got here.
PETE [*sitting left of bed*]: Yes.
LEN: They can't do enough for me here.
PETE: Why's that?
LEN: Because I'm no trouble. [MARK *sits right of bed.*] They
    treat me like a king. These nurses, they treat me exactly
    like a king. [*Pause.*] Mark looks as though he's caught a crab.
MARK: Do I?
PETE: Airy, this ward.

LEN: Best quality blankets, home cooking, everything you could wish for. Look at the ceiling. It's not too high and it's not too low.

[*Pause.*]

PETE: By the way, Mark, what happened to your pipe?

MARK: Nothing happened to it.

[*Pause.*]

LEN: You smoking a pipe? [*Pause.*] What's it like out today?

PETE: Bit chilly.

LEN: Bound to be.

PETE: The sun's come out.

LEN: The sun's come out? [*Pause.*] Well, Mark, bring off the treble chance this week?

MARK: Not me.

[*Pause.*]

LEN: Who's driving the tank?

PETE: What?

LEN: Who's driving the tank?

PETE: Don't ask me. We've been walking up the road back to back.

LEN: You've what? [*Pause.*] You've been walking up the road back to back? [*Pause.*] What are you doing sitting on my bed? You're not supposed to sit on the bed, you're supposed to sit on the chairs!

PETE [*rising and moving off*]: Well, give me a call when you get out. [*He exits.*]

MARK [*rising and following him*]: Yes give me a call. [*He exits.*]

LEN: [*calling after them*]: How do I know you'll be in?

Blackout. Lights come up on MARK'S *flat.* MARK *enters and sits.* PETE *enters, glances at* MARK, *sits.*

PETE: Horizontal personalities, those places. You're the only vertical. Makes you feel dizzy. [*Pause.*] You ever been inside one of those places?

MARK: I can't remember.

PETE: Right. [*Stubs out cigarette, rises, goes to exit.*]

MARK: All right. Why do you knock on my door?

PETE: What?

MARK: Come on. Why do you knock on my door?

PETE: What are you talking about?

MARK: Why?

PETE: I call to see you.

MARK: What do you want with me? Why come and see me?

PETE: Why?

MARK: You're playing a double game. You've been playing a double game. You've been using me. You've been leading me up the garden.

PETE: Mind how you go.

MARK: You've been wasting my time. For years.

PETE: Don't push me boy.

MARK: You think I'm a fool.

PETE: Is that what I think?

MARK: That's what you think. You think I'm a fool.

PETE: You are a fool.

MARK: You've always thought that.

PETE: From the beginning.

MARK: You've been leading me up the garden.

PETE: And you.

MARK: You know what you are? You're an infection.

PETE: Don't believe it. All I've got to do to destroy you is to leave you as you wish to be.

He walks out of the room. MARK *stares, slowly goes off as lights fade. Lights come up on down centre area. Enter* LEN.

LEN: They've stopped eating. It'll be a quick get out when the whistle blows. All their belongings are stacked in piles.

They've doused the fire. But I've heard nothing. What is the cause for alarm? Why is everything packed? Why are they ready for the off? But they say nothing. They've cut me off without a penny. And now they've settled down to a wide-eyed kip, crosslegged by the fire. It's insupportable. I'm left in the lurch. Not even a stale frankfurter, a slice of bacon rind, a leaf of cabbage, not even a mouldy piece of salami, like they used to sling me in the days when we told old tales by suntime. They sit, chock-full. But I smell a rat. They seem to be anticipating a rarer dish, a choicer spread. And this change. All about me the change. The yard as I know it is littered with scraps of cat's meat, pig bollocks, tin cans, bird brains, spare parts of all the little animals, a squelching, squealing carpet, all the dwarfs' leavings spittled in the muck, worms stuck in the poisoned shit heaps, the alleys a whirlpool of piss, slime, blood, and fruit juice. Now all is bare. All is clean. All is scrubbed. There is a lawn. There is a shrub. There is a flower.

The Collection

THE COLLECTION was first presented by Associated Rediffusion Television, London, on 11 May, 1961, with the following cast:

HARRY, *a man in his forties*	Griffith Jones
JAMES, *a man in his thirties*	Anthony Bate
STELLA, *a woman in her thirties*	Vivien Merchant
BILL, *a man in his late twenties*	John Ronane

Directed by Joan Kemp-Welch

The play was first presented on the stage at the Aldwych Theatre on 18 June 1962, with the following cast:

HARRY	Michael Hordern
JAMES	Kenneth Haigh
STELLA	Barbara Murray
BILL	John Ronane

Directed by Peter Hall and Harold Pinter

AUTUMN

The stage is divided into three areas, two peninsulas and a promontory. Each area is distinct and separate from the other.

Stage left, HARRY'S house in Belgravia. Elegant décor. Period furnishing. This set comprises the living-room, hall, front door and staircase to first floor. Kitchen exit below staircase.

Stage right, JAMES'S flat in Chelsea. Tasteful contemporary furnishing. This set comprises the living-room only. Offstage right, other rooms and front door.

Upstage centre on promontory, telephone box.

The telephone box is lit in a half light. A figure can be dimly observed inside it, with his back to the audience. The rest of the stage is dark. In the house the telephone is ringing. It is late at night.

Night light in house fades up. Street fades up.

HARRY *approaches the house, opens the front door and goes in. He switches on a light in the hall, goes into the living-room, walks to the telephone and lifts it.*

HARRY. Hullo.

VOICE. Is that you, Bill?

HARRY. No, he's in bed. Who's this?

VOICE. In bed?

HARRY. Who is this?

VOICE. What's he doing in bed?

Pause.

HARRY. Do you know it's four o'clock in the morning?

VOICE. Well, give him a nudge. Tell him I want a word with him. (*Pause.*)

HARRY. Who is this?

VOICE. Go and wake him up, there's a good boy. (*Pause.*)

HARRY. Are you a friend of his?

VOICE. He'll know me when he sees me.

HARRY. Oh yes?

Pause.

VOICE. Aren't you going to wake him?

HARRY. No, I'm not.

Pause.

VOICE. Tell him I'll be in touch.

The telephone cuts off. HARRY *replaces the receiver and stands still. The figure leaves the telephone box.* HARRY *walks slowly into the hall and up the stairs.*
Fade to blackout.
Fade up on flat. It is morning.
JAMES, *smoking, enters and sits on the sofa.*
STELLA *enters from a bedroom fixing a bracelet on her wrist. She goes to the cabinet, takes a perfume atomizer from her handbag and uses it on her throat and hands. She puts the atomizer into her bag and begins to put her gloves on.*

STELLA. I'm going.

Pause.

Aren't you coming in today?

Pause.

JAMES. No.
STELLA. You had to meet those people from . . .

Pause. She slowly walks to an armchair, picks up her jacket and puts it on.

You had to meet those people about that order. Shall I phone them when I get to the shop?
JAMES. You could do . . . yes.
STELLA. What are you going to do?

He looks at her, with a brief smile, then away.

Jimmy . . .

Pause.

Are you going out?

Pause.

Will you . . . be in tonight?

JAMES *reaches for a glass ashtray, flicks ash, and regards*

the ashtray. STELLA *turns and leaves the room. The front*
door slams. JAMES *continues regarding the ashtray.*
Fade to half light.
Fade up on house. Morning.
BILL *brings on a tray from the kitchen and places it on the*
table, arranges it, pours tea, sits, picks up a newspaper, reads,
drinks. HARRY, *in a dressing-gown, descends the stairs, trips,*
stumbles.

BILL (*turning*). What have you done?
HARRY. I tripped on that stair rod!

He comes into the room.

BILL. All right.
HARRY. It's that stair rod. I thought you said you were going
   to fix it.
BILL. I did fix it.
HARRY. Well, you didn't fix it very well.

He sits, holding his head.

Ooh.

BILL *pours tea for him.*
In the flat, JAMES *stubs his cigarette and goes out. The*
lights in the flat fade out.
HARRY *sips the tea, then puts the cup down.*

Where's my fruit juice? I haven't had my fruit juice.

BILL *regards the fruit juice on the tray.*

What's it doing over there?

BILL *gives it to him.* HARRY *sips it.*

What's this? Pineapple?

BILL. Grapefruit.

Pause.

HARRY. I'm sick and tired of that stair rod. Why don't you screw it in or something? You're supposed . . . you're supposed to be able to use your hands.

Pause.

BILL. What time did you get in?
HARRY. Four.
BILL. Good party?

Pause.

HARRY. You didn't make any toast this morning.
BILL. No. Do you want some?
HARRY. No. I don't.
BILL. I can if you like.
HARRY. It's all right. Don't bother.

Pause.

How are you spending your day today?
BILL. Go and see a film, I think.
HARRY. Wonderful life you lead. (*Pause.*) Do you know some maniac telephoned you last night?

BILL *looks at him.*

Just as I got in. Four o'clock. Walked in the door and the telephone was ringing.
BILL. Who was it?
HARRY. I've no idea.
BILL. What did he want?
HARRY. You. He was shy, wouldn't tell me his name.
BILL. Huh.

Pause.

HARRY. Who could it have been?
BILL. I've no idea.
HARRY. He was very insistent. Said he was going to get in touch again. (*Pause.*) Who the hell was it?

BILL. I've just said . . . I haven't the remotest idea.

Pause.

HARRY. Did you meet anyone last week?

BILL. Meet anyone? What do you mean?

HARRY. I mean could it have been anyone you met? You must have met lots of people.

BILL. I didn't speak to a soul.

HARRY. Must have been miserable for you.

BILL. I was only there one night, wasn't I? Some more?

HARRY. No, thank you.

> BILL *pours tea for himself.*
> *The telephone box fades up to half light, disclosing a figure entering it.*

I must shave.

> HARRY *sits, looking at* BILL, *who is reading the paper After a moment* BILL *looks up.*

BILL. Mmnnn?

> *Silence.* HARRY *stands, leaves the room and exits up the stairs, treading carefully over the stair rod.* BILL *reads the paper. The telephone rings.*
> BILL *lifts the receiver.*

Hullo.

VOICE. Is that you, Bill?

BILL. Yes?

VOICE. Are you in?

BILL. Who's this?

VOICE. Don't move. I'll be straight round.

BILL. What do you mean? Who is this?

VOICE. About two minutes. All right?

BILL. You can't do that. I've got some people here.

VOICE. Never mind. We can go into another room.

BILL. This is ridiculous. Do I know you?

VOICE. You'll know me when you see me.

BILL. Do you know me?

VOICE. Just stay where you are. I'll be right round.

BILL. But what do you want, who – ? You can't do that. I'm going straight out. I won't be in.

VOICE. See you.

The phone cuts off. BILL *replaces the receiver.*
The lights on the telephone box fade as the figure comes out and exits left.
BILL *puts on his jacket, goes into the hall, puts on his over-coat, swift but not hurried, opens the front door, and goes out. He exits up right.* HARRY'S *voice from upstairs.*

HARRY. Bill, was that you?

He appears at the head of the stairs.

Bill!

He goes downstairs, into the living-room, stands, observes the tray, and takes the tray into the kitchen.
JAMES *comes from up left in the street and looks at the house.*
HARRY *comes out of the kitchen, goes into the hall and up the stairs.*
JAMES *rings the bell.*
HARRY *comes down the stairs and opens the door.*

Yes?

JAMES. I'm looking for Bill Lloyd.

HARRY. He's out. Can I help?

JAMES. When will he be in?

HARRY. I can't say. Does he know you?

JAMES. I'll try some other time then.

HARRY. Well, perhaps you'd like to leave your name. I can tell him when I see him.

JAMES. No, that's all right. Just tell him I called.

HARRY. Tell him who called?

JAMES. Sorry to bother you.

HARRY. Just a minute. (JAMES *turns back*.) You're not the man who telephoned last night, are you?

JAMES. Last night?

HARRY. You didn't telephone early this morning?

JAMES. No . . . sorry . . .

HARRY. Well, what do you want?

JAMES. I'm looking for Bill.

HARRY. You didn't by any chance telephone just now?

JAMES. I think you've got the wrong man.

HARRY. I think you have.

JAMES. I don't think you know anything about it.

> JAMES *turns and goes.* HARRY *stands watching him.*
> *Fade to blackout.*
> *Fade up moonlight in flat.*
> *The front door closes, in flat.*
> STELLA *comes in, stands, switches on a lamp. She turns in the direction of the other rooms.*

STELLA. Jimmy?

> *Silence.*
> *She takes her gloves off, puts her handbag down, and is still. She goes to the record player, and puts on a record. It is 'Charlie Parker'. She listens, then exists to the bedroom.*
> *Fade up house. Night.*
> BILL *enters the living-room from the kitchen with magazines. He throws them in the hearth, goes to the drinks table and pours a drink, then lies on the floor with a drink by the hearth, flicking through a magazine.* STELLA *comes back into the room with a white Persian kitten. She lies back on the sofa, nuzzling it.* HARRY *comes downstairs, glances in at* BILL, *exits and walks down the street to up right.* JAMES *appears at the front door of the house from up left, looks after*

HARRY, *and rings the bell.* BILL *stands, and goes to the door.*
Fade flat to half light and music out.

BILL. Yes?

JAMES. Bill Lloyd?

BILL. Yes?

JAMES. Oh, I'd . . . I'd like to have a word with you.

Pause.

BILL. I'm sorry, I don't think I know you?

JAMES. Don't you?

BILL. No.

JAMES. Well, there's something I'd like to talk to you about

BILL. I'm terribly sorry, I'm busy.

JAMES. It won't take long.

BILL. I'm awfully sorry. Perhaps you'd like to put it down on paper and send it to me.

JAMES. That's not possible.

Pause.

BILL (*closing door*). Do forgive me –

JAMES (*foot in door*). Look. I want to speak to you.

Pause.

BILL. Did you phone me today?

JAMES. That's right. I called, but you'd gone out.

BILL. You called here? I didn't know that.

JAMES. I think I'd better come in, don't you?

BILL. You can't just barge into someone's house like this, you know. What do you want?

JAMES. Why don't you stop wasting your time and let me in?

BILL. I could call the police.

JAMES. Not worth it.

They stare at each other.

BILL. All right.

> JAMES *goes in.* BILL *closes the door.* JAMES *goes through the hall and into the living-room.* BILL *follows.* JAMES *looks about the room.*

JAMES. Got any olives?

BILL. How did you know my name?

JAMES. No olives?

BILL. Olives? I'm afraid not.

JAMES. You mean to say you don't keep olives for your guests?

BILL. You're not my guest, you're an intruder. What can I do for you?

JAMES. Do you mind if I sit down?

BILL. Yes, I do.

JAMES. You'll get over it.

> JAMES *sits.* BILL *stands.* JAMES *stands, takes off his overcoat, throws it on an armchair, and sits again.*

BILL. What's your name, old boy?

> JAMES *reaches to a bowl of fruit and breaks off a grape, which he eats.*

JAMES. Where shall I put the pips?

BILL. In your wallet.

> JAMES *takes out his wallet and deposits the pips. He regards* BILL.

JAMES. You're not a bad-looking bloke.

BILL. Oh, thanks.

JAMES. You're not a film star, but you're quite tolerable looking, I suppose.

BILL. That's more than I can say for you.

JAMES. I'm not interested in what you can say for me.

BILL. To put it quite bluntly, old chap, I'm even less interested than you are. Now look, come on please, what do you want?

JAMES *stands, walks to the drinks table and stares at the bottles. In the flat,* STELLA *rises with the kitten and goes off slowly, nuzzling it. The flat fades to blackout.* JAMES *pours himself a whisky.*

Cheers.

JAMES. Did you have a good time in Leeds last week?

BILL. What?

JAMES. Did you have a good time in Leeds last week?

BILL. Leeds?

JAMES. Did you enjoy yourself?

BILL. What makes you think I was in Leeds.

JAMES. Tell me all about it. See much of the town? Get out to the country at all?

BILL. What are you talking about?

Pause.

JAMES (*with fatigue*). Aaah. You were down there for the dress collection. You took some of your models.

BILL. Did I?

JAMES. You stayed at the Westbury Hotel.

BILL. Oh?

JAMES. Room 142.

BILL. 142? Oh. Was it comfortable?

JAMES. Comfortable enough.

BILL. Oh, good.

JAMES. Well, you had your yellow pyjamas with you.

BILL. Did I really? What, the ones with the black initials?

JAMES. Yes, you had them on you in 165.

BILL. In what?

JAMES. 165.

BILL. 165? I thought I was in 142.

JAMES. You booked into 142. But you didn't stay there.

BILL. Well, that's a bit silly, isn't it? Booking a room and not staying in it?

JAMES. 165 is just along the passage to 142; you're not far away.

BILL. Oh well, that's a relief.

JAMES. You could easily nip back to shave.

BILL. From 165?

JAMES. Yes.

BILL. What was I doing there?

JAMES (*casually*). My wife was in there. That's where you slept with her.

Silence.

BILL. Well . . . who told you that?

JAMES. She did.

BILL. You should have her seen to.

JAMES. Be careful.

BILL. Mmmm? Who is your wife?

JAMES. You know her.

BILL. I don't think so.

JAMES. No?

BILL. No, I don't think so at all.

JAMES. I see.

BILL. I was nowhere near Leeds last week, old chap. Nowhere near your wife either, I'm quite sure of that. Apart from that, I . . . just don't do such things. Not in my book.

Pause.

I wouldn't dream of it. Well, I think that closes that subject, don't you?

JAMES. Come here. I want to tell you something.

BILL. I'm expecting guests in a minute, you know. Cocktails, I'm standing for Parliament next season.

JAMES. Come here.

BILL. I'm going to be Minister for Home Affairs.

JAMES *moves to him.*

JAMES (*confidentially*). When you treat my wife like a whore, then I think I'm entitled to know what you've got to say about it.

BILL. But I don't know your wife.

JAMES. You do. You met her at ten o'clock last Friday in the lounge. You fell into conversation, you bought her a couple of drinks, you went upstairs together in the lift. In the lift you never took your eyes from her, you found you were both on the same floor, you helped her out, by her arm. You stood with her in the corridor, looking at her. You touched her shoulder, said good night, went to your room, she went to hers, you changed into your yellow pyjamas and black dressing-gown, you went down the passage and knocked on her door, you'd left your toothpaste in town. She opened the door, you went in, she was still dressed. You admired the room, it was so feminine, you felt awake, didn't feel like sleeping, you sat down, on the bed. She wanted you to go, you wouldn't. She became upset, you sympathized, away from home, on a business trip, horrible life, especially for a woman, you comforted her, you gave her solace, you stayed.

Pause.

BILL. Look, do you mind . . . just going off now. You're giving me a bit of a headache.

JAMES. You knew she was married . . . why did you feel it necessary . . . to do that?

BILL. She must have known she was married, too. Why did she feel it necessary . . . to do that?

Pause.

(*With a chuckle.*) That's got you, hasn't it?

Pause.

Well, look, it's really just a lot of rubbish. You know that.

BILL *goes to the cigarette box and lights a cigarette.*

Is she supposed to have resisted me at all?

JAMES. A little.

BILL. Only a little?

JAMES. Yes.

BILL. Do you believe her?

JAMES. Yes.

BILL. Everything she says?

JAMES. Sure.

BILL. Did she bite at all?

JAMES. No.

BILL. Scratch?

JAMES. A little.

BILL. You've got a devoted wife, haven't you? Keeps you well informed, right up to the minutest detail. She scratched a little, did she? Where? (*Holds up a hand.*) On the hand? No scar. No scar anywhere. Absolutely unscarred. We can go before a commissioner of oaths, if you like. I'll strip, show you my unscarred body. Yes, what we need is an independent witness. You got any chambermaids on your side or anything?

JAMES *applauds briefly.*

JAMES. You're a wag, aren't you? I never thought you'd be such a wag. You've really got a sense of fun. You know what I'd call you?

BILL. What?

JAMES. A wag.

BILL. Oh, thanks very much.

JAMES. No, I'm glad to pay a compliment when a compliment's due. What about a drink?

BILL. That's good of you.

JAMES. What will you have?

BILL. Got any vodka?

JAMES. Let's see. Yes, I think we can find you some vodka.

BILL. Oh, scrumptious.

JAMES. Say that again.

BILL. What?

JAMES. That word.

BILL. What, scrumptious?

JAMES. That's it.

BILL. Scrumptious.

JAMES. Marvellous. You probably remember that from school, don't you?

BILL. Now that you mention it I think you might be right.

JAMES. I thought I was. Here's your vodka.

BILL. That's very generous of you.

JAMES. Not at all. Cheers. (*They drink.*)

BILL. Cheers.

JAMES. Eh, come here.

BILL. What?

JAMES. I bet you're a wow at parties.

BILL. Well, it's nice of you to say so, but I wouldn't say I was all that much of a wow.

JAMES. Go on, I bet you are. (*Pause.*)

BILL. You think I'm a wow, do you?

JAMES. At parties I should think you are.

BILL. No, I'm not much of a wow really. The bloke I share this house with is, though.

JAMES. Oh, I met him. Looked a jolly kind of chap.

BILL. Yes, he's very good at parties. Bit of a conjurer.

JAMES. What, rabbits?

BILL. Well, not so much rabbits, no.

JAMES. No rabbits?

BILL. No. He doesn't like rabbits, actually. They give him hay fever.

JAMES. Poor chap.

BILL. Yes, it's a pity.

JAMES. Seen a doctor about it?

BILL. Oh, he's had it since he was that high.

JAMES. Brought up in the country, I suppose?

BILL. In a manner of speaking, yes.

Pause.

Ah well, it's been very nice meeting you, old chap. You must come again when the weather's better.

JAMES *makes a sudden move forward.* BILL *starts back, and falls over a pouffe on to the floor.* JAMES *chuckles. Pause.*

You've made me spill my drink. You've made me spill it on my cardigan.

JAMES *stands over him.*

I could easily kick you from here.

Pause.

Are you going to let me get up?

Pause.

Are you going to let me get up?

Pause.

Now listen . . . I'll tell you what . . .

Pause.

If you let me get up . .

Pause.

I'm not very comfortable.

Pause.

If you let me get up . . . I'll . . . I'll tell you . . . the truth . . .

Pause.

JAMES. Tell me the truth from there.
BILL. No. No, when I'm up.

JAMES. Tell me from there.

Pause.

BILL. Oh well. I'm only telling you because I'm utterly bored
... The truth ... is that it never happened ... what you
said, anyway. I didn't know she was married. She never
told me. Never said a word. But nothing of that ... happened, I can assure you. All that happened was ... you
were right, actually, about going up in the lift ... we ...
got out of the lift, and then suddenly she was in my arms.
Really wasn't my fault, nothing was further from my mind,
biggest surprise of my life, must have found me terribly
attractive quite suddenly, I don't know ... but I ... I
didn't refuse. Anyway, we just kissed a bit, only a few
minutes, by the lift, no one about, and that was that – she
went to her room.

He props himself up on the pouffe.

The rest of it just didn't happen. I mean, I wouldn't do
that sort of thing. I mean, that sort of thing ... it's just
meaningless. I can understand that you're upset, of course,
but honestly, there was nothing else to it. Just a few kisses.
(BILL *rises, wiping his cardigan.*) I'm dreadfully sorry, really,
I mean, I've no idea why she should make up all that.
Pure fantasy. Really rather naughty of her. Rather alarming.
(*Pause.*) Do you know her well?

JAMES. And then about midnight you went into her private
bathroom and had a bath. You sang 'Coming through the
Rye'. You used her bath towel. Then you walked about the
room with her bath towel, pretending you were a Roman.

BILL. Did I?

JAMES. Then I phoned.

Pause.

I spoke to her. Asked her how she was. She said she was

all right. Her voice was a little low. I asked her to speak up.
She didn't have much to say. You were sitting on the bed,
next to her.

Silence.

BILL. Not sitting. Lying.

Blackout.
Church bells.
Full light up on both the flat and the house.
Sunday morning.
*JAMES is sitting alone in the living-room of the flat, reading
the paper. HARRY and BILL are sitting in the living-room
of the house, coffee before them. BILL is reading the
paper.*
HARRY is watching him.
Silence.
Church bells.
Silence.

HARRY. Put that paper down.
BILL. What?
HARRY. Put it down.
BILL. Why?
HARRY. You've read it.
BILL. No, I haven't. There's lots to read, you know.
HARRY. I told you to put it down.

BILL looks at him, throws the paper at him coolly and rises.
HARRY picks it up and reads.

BILL. Oh, you just wanted it yourself, did you?
HARRY. Want it? I don't want it.

HARRY crumples the paper deliberately and drops it.

I don't want it. Do you want it?
BILL. You're being a little erratic this morning, aren't you?

HARRY. Am I?

BILL. I would say you were.

HARRY. Well, you know what it is, don't you?

BILL. No.

HARRY. It's the church bells. You know how church bells
    always set me off. You know how they affect me.

BILL. I never hear them.

HARRY. You're not the sort of person who would, are you?

BILL. I'm finding all this faintly idiotic.

> BILL *bends to pick up the paper.*

HARRY. Don't touch that paper.

BILL. Why not?

HARRY. Don't touch it.

> BILL *stares at him and then slowly picks it up.*
> *Silence.*
> *He tosses it to* HARRY.

BILL. You have it. I don't want it.

> BILL *goes out and up the stairs.* HARRY *opens the paper and*
> *reads it.*
> *In the flat,* STELLA *comes in with a tray of coffee and*
> *biscuits. She places the tray on the coffee-table and passes a*
> *cup to* JAMES. *She sips.*

STELLA. Would you like a biscuit?

JAMES. No, thank you.

> *Pause.*

STELLA. I'm going to have one.

JAMES. You'll get fat.

STELLA. From biscuits?

JAMES. You don't want to get fat, do you?

STELLA. Why not?

JAMES. Perhaps you do.

STELLA. It's not one of my aims.
JAMES. What is your aim?

Pause.

I'd like an olive.
STELLA. Olive? We haven't got any.
JAMES. How do you know?
STELLA. I know.
JAMES. Have you looked?
STELLA. I don't need to look, do I? I know what I've got.
JAMES. You know what you've got?

Pause.

Why haven't we got any olives?
STELLA. I didn't know you liked them.
JAMES. That must be the reason why we've never had them
   in the house. You've simply never been interested enough
   in olives to ask whether I liked them or not.

   The telephone rings in the house. HARRY *puts the paper
   down and goes to it.* BILL *comes down the stairs. They stop,
   facing each other, momentarily.* HARRY *lifts the receiver.*
   BILL *walks into the room, picks up the paper and sits.*

HARRY. Hullo. What? No. Wrong number. (*Replaces receiver.*)
   Wrong number. Who do you think it was?
BILL. I didn't think.
HARRY. Oh, by the way, a chap called for you yesterday.
BILL. Oh yes?
HARRY. Just after you'd gone out.
BILL. Oh yes?
HARRY. Ah well, time for the joint. Roast or chips?
BILL. I don't want any potatoes, thank you.
HARRY. No potatoes? What an extraordinary thing. Yes, this
   chap, he was asking for you, he wanted you.
BILL. What for?

HARRY. He wanted to know if you ever cleaned your shoes with furniture polish.

BILL. Really? How odd.

HARRY. Not odd. Some kind of national survey.

BILL. What did he look like?

HARRY. Oh . . . lemon hair, nigger brown teeth, wooden leg, bottlegreen eyes and a toupee. Know him?

BILL. Never met him.

HARRY. You'd know him if you saw him.

BILL. I doubt it.

HARRY. What, a man who looked like that?

BILL. Plenty of men look like that.

HARRY. That's true. That's very true. The only thing is that this particular man was here last night.

BILL. Was he? I didn't see him.

HARRY. Oh yes, he was here, but I've got a funny feeling he wore a mask. It was the same man, but he wore a mask, that's all there is to it. He didn't dance here last night, did he, or do any gymnastics?

BILL. No one danced here last night.

HARRY. Aah. Well, that's why you didn't notice his wooden leg. I couldn't help seeing it myself when he came to the front door because he stood on the top step stark naked. Didn't seem very cold, though. He had a waterbottle under his arm instead of a hat.

BILL. Those church bells have certainly left their mark on you.

HARRY. They haven't helped, but the fact of the matter is, old chap, that I don't like strangers coming into my house without an invitation. (*Pause.*) Who is this man and what does he want?

Pause. BILL *rises.*

BILL. Will you excuse me? I really think it's about time I was dressed, don't you?

BILL *goes up the stairs.*
HARRY, *after a moment, turns and follows. He slowly ascends the stairs.*
Fade to blackout on house.
In the flat JAMES *is still reading the paper.* STELLA *is sitting silently.*
Silence.

STELLA. What do you think about going for a run today . . . in the country?

Pause. JAMES *puts the paper down.*

JAMES. I've come to a decision.
STELLA. What?
JAMES. I'm going to go and see him.
STELLA. See him? Who? (*Pause.*) What for?
JAMES. Oh . . . have a chat with him.
STELLA. What's the point of doing that?
JAMES. I feel I'd like to.
STELLA. I just don't see . . . what there is to be gained. What's the point of it?

Pause.

What are you going to do, hit him?
JAMES. No, no. I'd just like to hear what he's got to say.
STELLA. Why?
JAMES. I want to know what his attitude is.

Pause.

STELLA. He doesn't matter.
JAMES. What do you mean?
STELLA. He's not important.
JAMES. Do you mean anyone would have done? You mean it just happened to be him, but it might as well have been anyone?

STELLA. No.

JAMES. What then?

STELLA. Of course it couldn't have been anyone. It was him. It was just . . . something . . .

JAMES. That's what I mean. It was him. That's why I think he's worth having a look at. I want to see what he's like It'll be instructive, educational.

Pause.

STELLA. Please don't go and see him. You don't know where he lives, anyway.

JAMES. You don't think I should see him?

STELLA. It won't . . . make you feel any better.

JAMES. I want to see if he's changed.

STELLA. What do you mean?

JAMES. I want to see if he's changed from when I last saw him. He may have gone down the drain since I last saw him. I must say he looked in good shape, though.

STELLA. You've never seen him.

Pause.

You don't know him.

Pause.

You don't know where he lives?

Pause.

When did you see him?

JAMES. We had dinner together last night.

STELLA. What?

JAMES. Splendid host.

STELLA. I don't believe it.

JAMES. Ever been to his place?

Pause.

Rather nice. Ever been there?

STELLA. I met him in Leeds, that's all.

JAMES. Oh, is that all. Well, we'll have to go round there one night. The grub's good, I can't deny it. I found him quite charming.

Pause.

He remembered the occasion well. He was perfectly frank. You know, a man's man. Straight from the shoulder. He entirely confirmed your story.

STELLA. Did he?

JAMES. Mmm. Only thing . . . he rather implied that you led him on. Typical masculine thing to say, of course.

STELLA. That's a lie.

JAMES. You know what men are. I reminded him that you'd resisted, and you'd hated the whole thing, but that you'd been – how can we say – somehow hypnotized by him, it happens sometimes. He agreed it can happen sometimes. He told me he'd been hypnotized once by a cat. Wouldn't go into any more details, though. Still, I must admit we rather hit it off. We've got the same interests. He was most amusing over the brandy.

STELLA. I'm not interested.

JAMES. In fact, he was most amusing over the whole thing.

STELLA. Was he?

JAMES. But especially over the brandy. He's got the right attitude, you see. As a man, I can only admire it.

STELLA. What is his attitude?

JAMES. What's your attitude?

STELLA. I don't know what you're . . . I just don't know what you're . . . I just . . . hoped you'd understand . . .

She covers her face, crying.

JAMES. Well, I do understand, but only after meeting him. Now I'm perfectly happy. I can see it both ways, three ways, all ways . . . every way. It's perfectly clear, there's nothing to it, everything's back to normal. The only difference is that I've come across a man I can respect. It isn't often you can do that, that that happens, and really I suppose I've got you to thank.

He bends forward and pats her arm.

Thanks.

Pause.

He reminds me of a bloke I went to school with. Hawkins. Honestly, he reminded me of Hawkins. Hawkins was an opera fan, too. So's what's-his-name. I'm a bit of an opera fan myself. Always kept it a dead secret. I might go along with your bloke to the opera one night. He says he can always get free seats. He knows quite a few of that crowd. Maybe I can track old Hawkins down and take him along, too. He's a very cultivated bloke, your bloke, quite a considerable intelligence at work there, I thought. He's got a collection of Chinese pots stuck on a wall, must have cost at least fifteen hundred a piece. Well, you can't help noticing that sort of thing. I mean, you couldn't say he wasn't a man of taste. He's brimming over with it. Well, I suppose he must have struck you the same way. No, really, I think I should thank you, rather than anything else. After two years of marriage it looks as though, by accident, you've opened up a whole new world for me.

Fade to blackout.
Fade up house. Night.
BILL *comes in from the kitchen with a tray of olives, cheese, crisps, and a transistor radio, playing Vivaldi, very quietly. He puts the tray on the table, arranges the cushions and eats a crisp.* JAMES *appears at the front door and rings the bell.* BILL *goes to the door, opens it, amd* JAMES *comes in. In the hall he helps* JAMES *off with his coat.*

JAMES *comes into the room,* BILL *follows.* JAMES *notices the tray with the olives, and smiles.* BILL *smiles.* JAMES *goes up to the Chinese vases and examines them.* BILL *pours drinks. In the flat the telephone rings.*
Fade up on flat. Night.
Fade up half light on telephone box.
A figure can be dimly seen in the telephone box. STELLA *enters from the bedroom, holding the kitten. She goes to the telephone.* BILL *gives* JAMES *a glass. They drink.*

STELLA. Hullo.
HARRY. Is that you, James?
STELLA. What? No, it isn't. Who's this?
HARRY. Where's James?
STELLA. He's out.
HARRY. Out? Oh, well, all right. I'll be straight round.
STELLA. What are you talking about? Who are you?
HARRY. Don't go out.

The telephone cuts off. STELLA *replaces the receiver and sits upright with the kitten on the chair.*
Fade to half light on flat.
Fade telephone box.

JAMES. You know something? You remind me of a chap I knew once. Hawkins. Yes. He was quite a tall lad.
BILL. Tall, was he?
JAMES. Yes.
BILL. Now why should I remind you of him?
JAMES. He was quite a card. (*Pause.*)
BILL. Tall, was he?
JAMES. That's . . . what he was.
BILL. Well, you're not short.
JAMES. I'm not tall.
BILL. Quite broad.
JAMES. That doesn't make me tall.

BILL. I never said it did.

JAMES. Well, what are you saying?

BILL. Nothing. (*Pause.*)

JAMES. I wouldn't exactly say I was broad, either.

BILL. Well, you only see yourself in the mirror, don't you?

JAMES. That's good enough for me.

BILL. They're deceptive.

JAMES. Mirrors?

BILL. Very.

JAMES. Have you got one?

BILL. What?

JAMES. A mirror.

BILL. There's one right in front of you.

JAMES. So there is.

> JAMES *looks into the mirror.*

Come here. You look in it, too.

> BILL *stands by him and looks. They look together, and then* JAMES *goes to the left of the mirror, and looks again at* BILL'S *reflection.*

I don't think mirrors are deceptive.

> JAMES *sits.* BILL *smiles, and turns up the radio. They sit listening.*
> *Fade to half light on house and radio out.*
> *Fade up full on flat.*
> *Doorbell.*
> STELLA *rises and goes off to the front door. The voices are heard off.*

STELLA. Yes?

HARRY. How do you do. My name's Harry Kane. I wonder if I might have a word with you. There's no need to be alarmed. May I come in?

STELLA. Yes.

HARRY (*entering*). In here?
STELLA. Yes.

They come into the room.

HARRY. What a beautiful lamp.
STELLA. What can I do for you?
HARRY. Do you know Bill Lloyd?
STELLA. No.
HARRY. Oh, you don't?
STELLA. No.
HARRY. You don't know him personally?
STELLA. I don't, no.
HARRY. I found him in a slum, you know, by accident. Just happened to be in a slum one day and there he was. I realized he had talent straight away. I gave him a roof, gave him a job, and he came up trumps. We've been close friends for years.
STELLA. Oh yes?
HARRY. You know of him, of course, don't you, by repute? He's a dress designer.
STELLA. I know of him.
HARRY. You're both dress designers.
STELLA. Yes.
HARRY. You don't belong to the Rags and Bags Club, do you?
STELLA. The what?
HARRY. The Rags and Bags Club. I thought I might have seen you down there.
STELLA. No, I don't know it.
HARRY. Shame. You'd like it.

Pause.

Yes.

Pause.

I've come about your husband.

STELLA. Oh?

HARRY. Yes. He's been bothering Bill recently, with some fantastic story.

STELLA. I know about it. I'm very sorry.

HARRY. Oh, you know? Well, it's really been rather disturbing. I mean, the boy has his work to get on with. This sort of thing spoils his concentration.

STELLA. I'm sorry. It's . . . very unfortunate.

HARRY. It is.

Pause.

STELLA. I can't understand it . . . We've been happily married for two years, you see. I've . . . been away before, you know . . . showing dresses, here and there, my husband runs the business. But it's never happened before.

HARRY. What hasn't?

STELLA. Well, that my husband has suddenly dreamed up such a fantastic story, for no reason at all.

HARRY. That's what I said it was. I said it was a fantastic story.

STELLA. It is.

HARRY. That's what I said and that's what Bill says. We both think it's a fantastic story.

STELLA. I mean, Mr. Lloyd was in Leeds, but I hardly saw him, even though we were staying in the same hotel. I never met him or spoke to him . . . and then my husband suddenly accused me of . . . it's really been very distressing.

HARRY. Yes. What do you think the answer is? Do you think your husband . . . doesn't trust you, or something?

STELLA. Of course he does – he's just not been very well lately, actually . . . overwork.

HARRY. That's bad. Still, you know what it's like in our business. Why don't you take him on a long holiday? South of France.

STELLA. Yes. I'm very sorry that Mr. Lloyd has had to put up with all this, anyway.

HARRY. Oh, what a beautiful kitten, what a really beautiful kitten. Kitty, kitty, kitty, what do you call her, come here, kitty, kitty.

> HARRY *sits next to* STELLA *and proceeds to pet and nuzzle the kitten.*
> *Fade flat to half light.*
> *Fade up full on house.*
> BILL *and* JAMES, *with drinks in the same position.*
> *Music comes up.* BILL *turns off the radio.*
> *Music out.*

BILL. Hungry?

JAMES. No.

BILL. Biscuit?

JAMES. I'm not hungry.

BILL. I've got some olives.

JAMES. Really?

BILL. Like one?

JAMES. No, thanks.

BILL. Why not?

JAMES. I don't like them.

> *Pause.*

BILL. Don't like olives?

> *Pause.*

What on earth have you got against olives?

> *Pause.*

JAMES. I detest them.

BILL. Really?

JAMES. It's the smell I hate.

> *Pause.*

BILL. Cheese? I've got a splendid cheese knife.

He picks up a cheese knife.

Look. Don't you think it's splendid?

JAMES. Is it sharp?

BILL. Try it. Hold the blade. It won't cut you. Not if you handle it properly. Not if you grasp it firmly up to the hilt.

> JAMES *does not touch the knife.*
> BILL *stands holding it.*
> *Lights in house remain.*
> *Fade up flat to full.*

HARRY (*standing*). Well, good-bye, I'm glad we've had our little chat.

STELLA. Yes.

HARRY. It's all quite clear now.

STELLA. I'm glad.

> *They move to the door.*

HARRY. Oh, Mr. Lloyd asked me if I would give you his best wishes . . . and sympathies.

> *He goes out. She stands still.*

Good-bye.

> *The front door closes.* STELLA *lies on the sofa with the kitten. She rests her head, is still.*
> *Fade flat to half light.*

BILL. What are you frightened of?

JAMES (*moving away*). What's that?

BILL. What?

JAMES. I thought it was thunder.

BILL (*to him*). Why are you frightened of holding this blade?

JAMES. I'm not frightened. I was just thinking of the thunder last week, when you and my wife were in Leeds.

BILL. Oh, not again, surely? I thought we'd left all that

behind. Surely we have? You're not still worried about that, are you?

JAMES. Oh no. Just nostalgia, that's all.

BILL. Surely the wound heals when you know the truth, doesn't it? I mean, when the truth is verified? I would have thought it did.

JAMES. Of course.

BILL. What's there left to think about? It's a thing regretted, never to be repeated. No past, no future. Do you see what I mean? You're a chap who's been married for two years, aren't you, happily? There's a bond of iron between you and your wife. It can't be corroded by a trivial thing like this. I've apologized, she's apologized. Honestly, what more can you want?

> *Pause.* JAMES *looks at him.* BILL *smiles.* HARRY *appears at the front door, opens and closes it quietly, and remains in the hall, unnoticed by the others.*

JAMES. Nothing.

BILL. Every woman is bound to have an outburst of . . . wild sensuality at one time or another. That's the way I look at it, anyway. It's part of their nature. Even though it may be the kind of sensuality of which you yourself have never been the fortunate recipient. What? (*He laughs.*) That is a husband's fate, I suppose. Mind you, I think it's the system that's at fault, not you. Perhaps she'll never need to do it again, who knows.

> JAMES *stands, goes to the fruit bowl, and picks up the fruit knife. He runs his finger along the blade.*

JAMES. This is fairly sharp.

BILL. What do you mean?

JAMES. Come on.

BILL. I beg your pardon?

JAMES. Come on. You've got that one. I've got this one.

BILL. What about it?

JAMES. I get a bit tired of words sometimes, don't you? Let's have a game. For fun.

BILL. What sort of game?

JAMES. Let's have a mock duel.

BILL. I don't want a mock duel, thank you.

JAMES. Of course you do. Come on. First one who's touched is a sissy.

BILL. This is all rather unsubtle, don't you think?

JAMES. Not in the least. Come on, into first position.

BILL. I thought we were friends.

JAMES. Of course we're friends. What on earth's the matter with you? I'm not going to kill you. It's just a game, that's all. We're playing a game. You're not windy, are you?

BILL. I think it's silly.

JAMES. I say, you're a bit of a spoilsport, aren't you?

BILL. I'm putting my knife down anyway.

JAMES. Well, I'll pick it up.

JAMES does so and faces him with two knives.

BILL. Now you've got two.

JAMES. I've got another one in my hip pocket.

Pause.

BILL. What do you do, swallow them?

JAMES. Do you?

Pause. They stare at each other.

(*Suddenly.*) Go on! Swallow it!

JAMES throws a knife at BILL's face. BILL throws up a hand to protect his face and catches the knife by the blade. It cuts his hand.

BILL. Ow!

JAMES. Well caught! What's the matter?

He examines BILL'S *hand.*

Let's have a look. Ah yes. Now you've got a scar on your hand. You didn't have one before, did you?

HARRY *comes into the room.*

HARRY (*entering*). What have you done, nipped your hand? Let's have a look. (*To* JAMES.) Only a little nip, isn't it? It's his own fault for not ducking. I must have told him dozens of times, you know, that if someone throws a knife at you the silliest thing you can do is to catch it. You're bound to hurt yourself, unless it's made of rubber. The safest thing to do is duck. You're Mr. Horne?

JAMES. That's right.

HARRY. I'm so glad to meet you. My name's Harry Kane. Bill been looking after you all right? I asked him to see that you stayed until I got back. So glad you could spare the time. What are we drinking? Whisky? Let's fill you up. You and your wife run that little boutique down the road, don't you? Funny we've never met, living so close, all in the same trade, eh? Here you are. Got one, Bill? Where's your glass? This one? Here . . . you are. Oh, stop rubbing your hand, for goodness' sake. It's only a cheese knife. Well, Mr. Horne, all the very best. Here's wishing us all health, happiness and prosperity in the time to come, not forgetting your wife, of course. Healthy minds in healthy bodies. Cheers.

They drink.

By the way, I've just seen your wife. What a beautiful kitten she has. You should see it, Bill; it's all white. We had a very pleasant chat, your wife and I. Listen . . . old chap . . . can I be quite blunt with you?

JAMES. Of course.

HARRY. Your wife . . . you see . . . made a little tiny confession to me. I think I can use that word.

Pause.

BILL *is sucking his hand.*

What she confessed was ... that she'd made the whole thing up. She'd made the whole damn thing up. For some odd reason of her own. They never met, you see, Bill and your wife; they never even spoke. This is what Bill says, and this is now what your wife admits. They had nothing whatever to do with each other; they don't know each other. Women are very strange. But I suppose you know more about that than I do; she's your wife. If I were you I'd go home and knock her over the head with a saucepan and tell her not to make up such stories again.

Pause.

JAMES. She made the whole thing up, eh?

HARRY. I'm afraid she did.

JAMES. I see. Well, thanks very much for telling me.

HARRY. I thought it would be clearer for you, coming from someone completely outside the whole matter.

JAMES. Yes. Thank you.

HARRY. Isn't that so, Bill?

BILL. Oh, quite so. I don't even know the woman. Wouldn't know her if I saw her. Pure fantasy.

JAMES. How's your hand?

BILL. Not bad.

JAMES. Isn't it strange that you confirmed the whole of her story?

BILL. It amused me to do so.

JAMES. Oh?

BILL. Yes. You amused me. You wanted me to confirm it. It amused me to do so.

Pause.

HARRY. Bill's a slum boy, you see, he's got a slum sense of

humour. That's why I never take him along with me to parties. Because he's got a slum mind. I have nothing against slum minds *per se*, you understand, nothing at all. There's a certain kind of slum mind which is perfectly all right in a slum, but when this kind of slum mind gets out of the slum it sometimes persists, you see, it rots everything. That's what Bill is. There's something faintly putrid about him, don't you find? Like a slug. There's nothing wrong with slugs in their place, but he's a slum slug; there's nothing wrong with slum slugs in their place, but this one won't keep his place – he crawls all over the walls of nice houses, leaving slime, don't you, boy? He confirms stupid sordid little stories just to amuse himself, while everyone else has to run round in circles to get to the root of the matter and smooth the whole thing out. All he can do is sit and suck his bloody hand and decompose like the filthy putrid slum slug he is. What about another whisky, Horne?

JAMES. No, I think I must be off now. Well, I'm glad to hear that nothing did happen. Great relief to me.

HARRY. It must be.

JAMES. My wife's not been very well lately, actually. Overwork.

HARRY. That's bad. Still, you know what it's like in our business.

JAMES. Best thing to do is take her on a long holiday, I think.

HARRY. South of France.

JAMES. The Isles of Greece.

HARRY. Sun's essential, of course.

JAMES. I know. Bermuda.

HARRY. Perfect.

JAMES. Well, thanks very much, Mr. Kane, for clearing my mind. I don't think I'll mention it when I get home. Take her out for a drink or something. Forget all about it.

HARRY. Better hurry up. It's nearly closing time.

JAMES *moves to* BILL, *who is sitting.*

JAMES. I'm very sorry I cut your hand. You're lucky you caught it, of course. Otherwise it might have cut your mouth. Still, it's not too bad, is it?

Pause.

Look . . . I really think I ought to apologize for this silly story my wife made up. The fault is really all hers, and mine, for believing her. You're not to blame for taking it as you did. The whole thing must have been an impossible burden for you. What do you say we shake hands, as a testimony of my goodwill?

JAMES *extends his hand.* BILL *rubs his hand but does not extend it.*

HARRY. Come on, Billy, I think we've had enough of this stupidity, don't you?

Pause.

BILL. I'll . . . tell you . . . the truth.

HARRY. Oh, for God's sake, don't be ridiculous. Come on, Mr. Horne, off you go now, back to your wife, old boy, leave this . . . tyke to me.

JAMES *does not move. He looks down at* BILL.

Come on, Jimmy, I think we've had enough of this stupidity don't you?

JAMES *looks at him sharply.*
HARRY *stops still.*

BILL. I never touched her . . . we sat . . . in the lounge, on a sofa . . . for two hours . . . talked . . . we talked about it . . . we didn't . . . move from the lounge . . . never went to her room . . . just talked . . . about what we would do

. . . if we did get to her room . . . two hours . . . we never touched . . . we just talked about it . . .

> *Long silence.*
> JAMES *leaves the house.*
> HARRY *sits.* BILL *remains sitting sucking his hand.*
> *Silence.*
> *Fade house to half light.*
> *Fade up full on flat.*
> STELLA *is lying with the kitten.*
> *The flat door closes.* JAMES *comes in. He stands looking at her.*

JAMES. You didn't do anything, did you?

> *Pause.*

He wasn't in your room. You just talked about it, in the lounge.

> *Pause.*

That's the truth, isn't it?

> *Pause.*

You just sat and talked about what you would do if you went to your room. That's what you did.

> *Pause.*

Didn't you?

> *Pause.*

That's the truth . . . isn't it?

> STELLA *looks at him, neither confirming nor denying. Her face is friendly, sympathetic.*
> *Fade flat to half light.*
> *The four figures are still, in the half light.*
> *Fade to blackout.*

Curtain

The Lover

THE LOVER was first presented by Associated-Rediffusion Television, London, March 28th, 1963, with the following cast:

RICHARD   Alan Badel
SARAH   Vivien Merchant
JOHN   Michael Forrest

Directed by Joan Kemp-Welch

The play was first presented on the stage by Michael Codron and David Hall at the Arts Theatre, September 18th, 1963, with the following cast:

RICHARD   Scott Forbes
SARAH   Vivien Merchant
JOHN   Michael Forrest

Directed by Harold Pinter

Assisted by Guy Vaesen

Summer. A detached house near Windsor

The stage consists of two areas. Living-room right, with small hall and front door up centre. Bedroom and balcony, on a level, left. There is a short flight of stairs to bedroom door. Kitchen off right. A table with a long velvet cover stands against the left wall of the living-room, centre stage. In the small hall there is a cupboard. The furnishings are tasteful, comfortable.

SARAH is emptying and dusting ashtrays in the living-room. It is morning. She wears a crisp, demure dress. RICHARD comes into the bedroom from bathroom, off left, collects his briefcase from hall cupboard, goes to SARAH, kisses her on the cheek. He looks at her for a moment smiling. She smiles.

RICHARD (*amiably*). Is your lover coming today?
SARAH. Mmnn.
RICHARD. What time?
SARAH. Three.
RICHARD. Will you be going out . . . or staying in?
SARAH. Oh . . . I think we'll stay in.
RICHARD. I thought you wanted to go to that exhibition.
SARAH. I did, yes . . . but I think I'd prefer to stay in with him today.
RICHARD. Mmn-hmmn. Well, I must be off.

He goes to the hall and puts on his bowler hat.

RICHARD. Will he be staying long do you think?
SARAH. Mmmmnnn . . .
RICHARD. About . . . six, then.
SARAH. Yes.
RICHARD. Have a pleasant afternoon.
SARAH. Mmnn.
RICHARD. Bye-bye.
SARAH. Bye.

He opens the front door and goes out. She continues dusting.
The lights fade.
Fade up. Early evening. SARAH *comes into room from kitchen.*
She wears the same dress, but is now wearing a pair of very
high-heeled shoes. She pours a drink and sits on chaise longue
with magazine. There are six chimes of the clock. RICHARD
comes in the front door. He wears a sober suit, as in the
morning. He puts his briefcase down in the hall and goes into
the room. She smiles at him and pours him a whisky.

Hullo.

RICHARD. Hullo.

He kisses her on the cheek. Takes glass, hands her the evening
paper and sits down left. She sits on chaise longue with paper.

Thanks.

He drinks, sits back and sighs with contentment.

Aah.

SARAH. Tired?

RICHARD. Just a little.

SARAH. Bad traffic?

RICHARD. No. Quite good traffic, actually.

SARAH. Oh, good.

RICHARD. Very smooth.

Pause.

SARAH. It seemed to me you were just a little late.

RICHARD. Am I?

SARAH. Just a little.

RICHARD. There was a bit of a jam on the bridge.

SARAH *gets up, goes to drinks table to collect her glass, sits*
again on the chaise longue.

Pleasant day?

SARAH. Mmn. I was in the village this morning.

RICHARD. Oh yes? See anyone?

SARAH. Not really, no. Had lunch.

RICHARD. In the village?

SARAH. Yes.

RICHARD. Any good?

SARAH. Quite fair. (*She sits.*)

RICHARD. What about this afternoon? Pleasant afternoon?

SARAH. Oh yes. Quite marvellous.

RICHARD. Your lover came, did he?

SARAH. Mmnn. Oh yes.

RICHARD. Did you show him the hollyhocks?

Slight pause.

SARAH. The hollyhocks?

RICHARD. Yes.

SARAH. No, I didn't.

RICHARD. Oh.

SARAH. Should I have done?

RICHARD. No, no. It's simply that I seem to remember your saying he was interested in gardening.

SARAH. Mmnn, yes, he is.

Pause.

Not all that interested, actually.

RICHARD. Ah.

Pause.

Did you go out at all, or did you stay in?

SARAH. We stayed in.

RICHARD. Ah. (*He looks up at the Venetian blinds.*) That blind hasn't been put up properly.

SARAH. Yes, it is a bit crooked, isn't it?

Pause.

RICHARD. Very sunny on the road. Of course, by the time I got on to it the sun was beginning to sink. But I imagine it was quite warm here this afternoon. It was warm in the City.

SARAH. Was it?

RICHARD. Pretty stifling. I imagine it was quite warm everywhere.

SARAH. Quite a high temperature, I believe.

RICHARD. Did it say so on the wireless?

SARAH. I think it did, yes.

Slight pause.

RICHARD. One more before dinner?

SARAH. Mmn.

He pours drinks.

RICHARD. I see you had the Venetian blinds down.

SARAH. We did, yes.

RICHARD. The light was terribly strong.

SARAH. It was. Awfully strong.

RICHARD. The trouble with this room is that it catches the sun so directly, when it's shining. You didn't move to another room?

SARAH. No. We stayed here.

RICHARD. Must have been blinding.

SARAH. It was. That's why we put the blinds down.

Pause.

RICHARD. The thing is it gets so awfully hot in here with the blinds down.

SARAH. Would you say so?

RICHARD. Perhaps not. Perhaps it's just that you feel hotter.

SARAH. Yes. That's probably it.

Pause.

What did you do this afternoon?

RICHARD. Long meeting. Rather inconclusive.

SARAH. It's a cold supper. Do you mind?

RICHARD. Not in the least.

SARAH. I didn't seem to have time to cook anything today.

She moves towards the kitchen.

RICHARD. Oh, by the way . . . I rather wanted to ask you something.

SARAH. What?

RICHARD. Does it ever occur to you that while you're spending the afternoon being unfaithful to me I'm sitting at a desk going through balance sheets and graphs?

SARAH. What a funny question.

RICHARD. No, I'm curious.

SARAH. You've never asked me that before.

RICHARD. I've always wanted to know.

Slight pause.

SARAH. Well, of course it occurs to me.

RICHARD. Oh, it does?

SARAH. Mmnn.

Slight pause.

RICHARD. What's your attitude to that, then?

SARAH. It makes it all the more piquant.

RICHARD. Does it really?

SARAH. Of course.

RICHARD. You mean while you're with him . . . you actualiy have a picture of me, sitting at my desk going through balance sheets?

SARAH. Only at . . . certain times.

RICHARD. Of course.

SARAH. Not all the time.

RICHARD. Well, naturally.

SARAH. At particular moments.

RICHARD. Mmnn. But, in fact, I'm not completely forgotten?

SARAH. Not by any means.

RICHARD. That's rather touching, I must admit.

Pause.

SARAH. How could I forget you?

RICHARD. Quite easily, I should think.

SARAH. But I'm in your house.

RICHARD. With another.

SARAH. But it's you I love.

RICHARD. I beg your pardon?

SARAH. But it's you I love.

Pause. He looks at her, proffers his glass.

RICHARD. Let's have another drink.

She moves forward. He withdraws his glass, looks at her shoes.

What shoes are they?

SARAH. Mmnn?

RICHARD. Those shoes. They're unfamiliar. Very high-heeled, aren't they?

SARAH (*muttering*). Mistake. Sorry.

RICHARD (*not hearing*). Sorry? I beg your pardon?

SARAH. I'll . . . take them off.

RICHARD. Not quite the most comfortable shoes for an evening at home, I would have thought.

She goes into hall, opens cupboard, puts high-heeled shoes into cupboard, puts on low-heeled shoes. He moves to drinks table, pours himself a drink. She moves to centre table, lights a cigarette.

So you had a picture of me this afternoon, did you, sitting in my office?

SARAH. I did, yes. It wasn't a terribly convincing one, though.

RICHARD. Oh, why not?

SARAH. Because I knew you weren't there. I knew you were with your mistress.

Pause.

RICHARD. Was I?

Short pause.

SARAH. Aren't you hungry?

RICHARD. I had a heavy lunch.

SARAH. How heavy?

He stands at the window.

RICHARD. What a beautiful sunset.

SARAH. Weren't you?

He turns and laughs.

RICHARD. What mistress?

SARAH. Oh, Richard . . .

RICHARD. No, no, it's simply the word that's so odd.

SARAH. Is it? Why?

Slight pause.

I'm honest with you, aren't I? Why can't you be honest with me?

RICHARD. But I haven't got a mistress. I'm very well acquainted with a whore, but I haven't got a mistress. There's a world of difference.

SARAH. A whore?

RICHARD (*taking an olive*). Yes. Just a common or garden slut. Not worth talking about. Handy between trains, nothing more.

SARAH. You don't travel by train. You travel by car.

RICHARD. Quite. A quick cup of while cocoa they're checking the oil and water.

Pause.

SARAH. Sounds utterly sterile

RICHARD. No.

Pause.

SARAH. I must say I never expected you to admit it so readily.

RICHARD. Oh, why not? You've never put it to me so bluntly before, have you? Frankness at all costs. Essential to a healthy marriage. Don't you agree?

SARAH. Of course.

RICHARD. You agree.

SARAH. Entirely.

RICHARD. I mean, you're utterly frank with me, aren't you?

SARAH. Utterly.

RICHARD. About your lover. I must follow your example.

SARAH. Thank you.

Pause.

Yes, I have suspected it for some time.

RICHARD. Have you really?

SARAH. Mmnn.

RICHARD. Perceptive.

SARAH. But, quite honestly, I can't really believe she's just . . . what you say.

RICHARD. Why not?

SARAH. It's just not possible. You have such taste. You care so much for grace and elegance in women.

RICHARD. And wit.

SARAH. And wit, yes.

RICHARD. Wit, yes. Terribly important, wit, for a man.

SARAH. Is she witty?

RICHARD (*laughing*). These terms just don't apply. You can't sensibly inquire whether a whore is witty. It's of no significance whether she is or she isn't. She's simply a whore, a functionary who either pleases or displeases.

SARAH. And she pleases you?

RICHARD. Today she is pleasing. Tomorrow . . .? One can't say.

He moves towards the bedroom door taking off his jacket.

SARAH. I must say I find your attitude to women rather alarming.

RICHARD. Why? I wasn't looking for your double, was I? I wasn't looking for a woman I could respect, as you, whom I could admire and love, as I do you. Was I? All I wanted was . . . how shall I put it . . . someone who could express and engender lust with all lust's cunning. Nothing more.

He goes into the bedroom, hangs his jacket up in the ward-robe, and changes into his slippers.
In the living-room SARAH puts her drink down, hesitates and then follows into the bedroom.

SARAH. I'm sorry your affair possesses so little dignity.

RICHARD. The dignity is in my marriage.

SARAH. Or sensibility.

RICHARD. The sensibility likewise. I wasn't looking for such attributes. I find them in you.

SARAH. Why did you look at all?

Slight pause.

RICHARD. What did you say?

SARAH. Why look . . . elsewhere . . . at all?

RICHARD. But my dear, you looked. Why shouldn't I look?

Pause.

SARAH. Who looked first?

RICHARD. You.

SARAH. I don't think that's true.

RICHARD. Who, then?

She looks at him with a slight smile.
Fade up. Night. Moonlight on balcony. The lights fade.
RICHARD *comes in bedroom door in his pyjamas. He picks up*
a book and looks at it. SARAH *comes from bathroom in her*
nightdress. There is a double bed. SARAH *sits at the dressing-*
table. Combs her hair.

SARAH. Richard?
RICHARD. Mnn?
SARAH. Do you ever think about me at all . . . when you're
   with her?
RICHARD. Oh, a little. Not much.

   Pause.

We talk about you.
SARAH. You talk about me with her?
RICHARD. Occasionally. It amuses her.
SARAH. Amuses her?
RICHARD (*choosing a book*). Mmnn.
SARAH. How . . . do you talk about me?
RICHARD. Delicately. We discuss you as we would play an
   antique music box. We play it for our titillation, whenever
   desired.

   Pause.

SARAH. I can't pretend the picture gives me great pleasure.
RICHARD. It wasn't intended to. The pleasure is mine.
SARAH. Yes, I see that, of course.
RICHARD (*sitting on the bed*). Surely your own afternoon
   pleasures are sufficient for you, aren't they? You don't
   expect extra pleasure from my pastimes, do you?
SARAH. No, not at all.
RICHARD. Then why all the questions?
SARAH. Well, it was you who started it. Asking me so many

questions about . . . my side of it. You don't normally do that.

RICHARD. Objective curiosity, that's all.

He touches her shoulders.

You're not suggesting I'm jealous, surely?

She smiles, stroking his hand.

SARAH. Darling. I know you'd never stoop to that.

RICHARD. Good God, no.

He squeezes her shoulder.

What about you? You're not jealous, are you?

SARAH. No. From what you tell me about your lady I seem to have a far richer time than you do.

RICHARD. Possibly.

He opens the windows fully and stands by them, looking out.

What peace. Come and look.

She joins him at the window.
They stand silently.

What would happen if I came home early one day, I wonder?

Pause.

SARAH. What would happen if I followed you one day, I wonder?

Pause.

RICHARD. Perhaps we could all meet for tea in the village.

SARAH. Why the village? Why not here?

RICHARD. Here? What an extraordinary remark.

Pause.

Your poor lover has never seen the night from this window, has he?

SARAH. No. He's obliged to leave before sunset, unfortunately.

RICHARD. Doesn't he get a bit bored with these damn afternoons? This eternal teatime? I would. To have as the
constant image of your lust a milk jug and teapot. Must be
terribly dampening.

SARAH. He's very adaptable. And, of course, when one puts
the blinds down it does become a kind of evening.

RICHARD. Yes, I suppose it would.

Pause.

What does he think of your husband?

Slight pause.

SARAH. He respects you.

Pause.

RICHARD. I'm rather moved by that remark, in a strange kind
of way. I think I can understand why you like him so
much.

SARAH. He's terribly sweet.

RICHARD. Mmn-hmmnn.

SARAH. Has his moods, of course.

RICHARD. Who doesn't?

SARAH. But I must say he's very loving. His whole body
emanates love.

RICHARD. How nauseating.

SARAH. No.

RICHARD. Manly with it, I hope?

SARAH. Entirely.

RICHARD. Sounds tedious.

SARAH. Not at all.

Pause.

He has a wonderful sense of humour.

RICHARD. Oh, jolly good. Makes you laugh, does he? Well,

mind the neighbours don't hear you. The last thing we want is gossip.

Pause.

SARAH. It's wonderful to live out here, so far away from the main road, so secluded.

RICHARD. Yes, I do agree.

They go back into the room. They get into the bed. He picks up his book and looks at it. He closes it and puts it down.

This isn't much good.

He switches off his bedside lamp. She does the same. Moonlight.

He's married, isn't he?

SARAH. Mmmmn.

RICHARD. Happily?

SARAH. Mmmmn.

Pause.

And you're happy, aren't you? You're not in any way jealous?

RICHARD. No.

SARAH. Good. Because I think things are beautifully balanced, Richard.

Fade.
Fade up. Morning. SARAH putting on her negligee in the bedroom. She begins to make the bed.

SARAH. Darling.

Pause.

Will the shears be ready this morning?

RICHARD (*in bathroom, off*). The what?

SARAH. The shears.

RICHARD. No, not this morning.

He enters, fully dressed in his suit. Kisses her on the cheek.

Not till Friday. Bye-bye.

He leaves the bedroom, collects hat and briefcase from hall.

SARAH. Richard.

He turns.

You won't be home too early today, will you?

RICHARD. Do you mean he's coming again today? Good gracious. He was here yesterday. Coming again today?

SARAH. Yes.

RICHARD. Oh. No, well, I won't be home early. I'll go to the National Gallery.

SARAH. Right.

RICHARD. Bye-bye.

SARAH. Bye.

The lights fade.
Fade up. Afternoon. SARAH *comes downstairs into living-room. She wears a very tight, low-cut black dress. She hastily looks at herself in the mirror. Suddenly notices she is wearing low-heeled shoes. She goes quickly to cupboard changes them for her high-heeled shoes. Looks again in mirror, smooths her hips. Goes to window, pulls venetian blinds down, opens them, and closes them until there is a slight slit of light. There are three chimes of a clock. She looks at her watch, goes towards the flowers on the table. Door bell. She goes to door. It is the milkman,* JOHN.

JOHN. Cream?

SARAH. You're very late.

JOHN. Cream?

SARAH. No, thank you.

JOHN. Why not?

SARAH. I have some. Do I owe you anything?

JOHN. Mrs. Owen just had three jars. Clotted.

SARAH. What do I owe you?

JOHN. It's not Saturday yet.

SARAH (*taking the milk*). Thank you.

JOHN. Don't you fancy any cream? Mrs. Owen had three jars.

SARAH. Thank you.

> *She closes the door. Goes into the kitchen with milk. Comes back with a tea-tray, holding teapot and cups, sets it on small table above chaise longue. She briefly attends to the flowers, sits on the chaise longue, crosses her legs, uncrosses them, puts her legs up on chaise longue, smooths her stockings under her skirt. The doorbell rings. Pulling her dress down she moves to the door, opens it.*

Hallo, Max.

> RICHARD *comes in. He is wearing a suede jacket, and no tie. He walks into the room and stands.*
>
> *She closes the door behind him. Walks slowly down past him, and sits on the chaise longue, crossing her legs.*
>
> *Pause.*
>
> *He moves slowly to chaise longue and stands very close to her at her back. She arches her back, uncrosses her legs, moves away to low chair down left.*
>
> *Pause.*
>
> *He looks at her, then moves towards the hall cupboard, brings out a bongo drum. He places the drum on the chaise longue, stands.*
>
> *Pause.*
>
> *She rises, moves past him towards the hall, turns, looks at him. He moves below chaise. They sit at either end. He begins to tap the drum. Her forefinger moves along drum towards his hand. She scratches the back of his hand sharply. Her hand retreats. Her fingers tap one after the other towards him, and*

rest. Her forefinger scratches between his fingers. Her other
fingers do the same. His legs tauten. His hand clasps hers.
Her hand tries to escape. Wild beats of their fingers tangling.
Stillness.
She gets up, goes to drinks table, lights a cigarette, moves to
window. He puts drum down on chair down right, picks up
cigarette, moves to her.

MAX. Excuse me.

> *She glances at him and away.*

Excuse me, have you got a light?

> *She does not respond.*

Do you happen to have a light?
SARAH. Do you mind leaving me alone?
MAX. Why?

> *Pause.*

I'm merely asking if you can give me a light.

> *She moves from him and looks up and down the room. He*
> *follows to her shoulder. She turns back.*

SARAH. Excuse me.

> *She moves past him. Close, his body follows.*
> *She stops.*

I don't like being followed.
MAX. Just give me a light and I won't bother you. That's all
I want.
SARAH (*through her teeth*). Please go away. I'm waiting for
someone.
MAX. Who?
SARAH. My husband.
MAX. Why are you so shy? Eh? Where's your lighter?

He touches her body. An indrawn breath from her.

Here?

Pause.

Where is it?

He touches her body. A gasp from her.

Here?

She wrenches herself away. He traps her in the corner.

SARAH (*hissing*). What do you think you're doing?
MAX. I'm dying for a puff.
SARAH. I'm waiting for my husband!
MAX. Let me get a light from yours.

They struggle silently.
She breaks away to wall.
Silence.
He approaches.

Are you all right, miss? I've just got rid of that . . . gentleman. Did he hurt you in any way?
SARAH. Oh, how wonderful of you. No, no, I'm all right. Thank you.
MAX. Very lucky I happened to be passing. You wouldn't believe that could happen in such a beautiful park.
SARAH. No, you wouldn't.
MAX. Still, you've come to no harm.
SARAH. I can never thank you enough. I'm terribly grateful, I really am.
MAX. Why don't you sit down a second and calm yourself.
SARAH. Oh, I'm quite calm – but . . . yes, thank you. You're so kind. Where shall we sit.
MAX. Well, we can't sit out. It's raining. What about that park-keeper's hut?

SARAH. Do you think we should? I mean, what about the park-keeper?

MAX. I am the park-keeper.

They sit on the chaise longue.

SARAH. I never imagined I could meet anyone so kind.

MAX. To treat a lovely young woman like you like that, it's unpardonable.

SARAH (*gazing at him*). You seem so mature, so . . . appreciative.

MAX. Of course.

SARAH. So gentle. So . . . Perhaps it was all for the best.

MAX. What do you mean?

SARAH. So that we could meet. So that we could meet. You and I.

Her fingers trace his thigh. He stares at them, lifts them off.

MAX. I don't quite follow you.

SARAH. Don't you?

Her fingers trace his thigh. He stares at them, lifts them off.

MAX. Now look, I'm sorry. I'm married.

She takes his hand and puts it on her knee.

SARAH. You're so sweet, you mustn't worry.

MAX (*snatching his hand away*). No, I really am. My wife's waiting for me.

SARAH. Can't you speak to strange girls?

MAX. No.

SARAH. Oh, how sickening you are. How tepid.

MAX. I'm sorry.

SARAH. You men are all alike. Give me a cigarette.

MAX. I bloody well won't.

SARAH. I beg your pardon?

MAX. Come here, Dolores.

SARAH. Oh no, not me. Once bitten twice shy, thanks. (*She stands.*) Bye-bye.

MAX. You can't get out, darling. The hut's locked. We're alone. You're trapped.

SARAH. Trapped! I'm a married woman. You can't treat me like this.

MAX (*moving to her*). It's teatime, Mary.

She moves swiftly behind the table and stands there with her back to the wall. He moves to the opposite end of the table, hitches his trousers, bends and begins to crawl under the table towards her.

He disappears under the velvet cloth. Silence. She stares down at the table. Her legs are hidden from view. His hand is on her leg. She looks about, grimaces, grits her teeth, gasps, gradually sinks under the table, and disappears. Long silence.

HER VOICE. Max!

Lights fade.
Fade up.
MAX sitting on chair down left.
SARAH pouring tea.

SARAH. Max.
MAX. What?
SARAH (*fondly*). Darling.

Slight pause.

What is it? You're very thoughtful.
MAX. No.
SARAH. You are. I know it.

Pause.

MAX. Where's your husband?

Pause.

SARAH. My husband? You know where he is.

MAX. Where?

SARAH. He's at work.

MAX. Poor fellow. Working away, all day.

Pause.

I wonder what he's like.

SARAH (*chuckling*). Oh, Max.

MAX. I wonder if we'd get on. I wonder if we'd . . . you know . . . hit it off.

SARAH. I shouldn't think so.

MAX. Why not?

SARAH. You've got very little in common.

MAX. Have we? He's certainly very accommodating. I mean, he knows perfectly well about these afternoons of ours, doesn't he?

SARAH. Of course.

MAX. He's known for years.

Slight pause.

Why does he put up with it?

SARAH. Why are you suddenly talking about him? I mean what's the point of it? It isn't a subject you normally elaborate on.

MAX. Why does he put up with it?

SARAH. Oh, shut up.

MAX. I asked you a question.

Pause.

SARAH. He doesn't mind.

MAX. Doesn't he?

Slight pause.

Well, I'm beginning to mind.

Pause.

SARAH. What did you say.
MAX. I'm beginning to mind.

Slight pause.

It's got to stop. It can't go on.
SARAH. Are you serious?

Silence.

MAX. It can't go on.
SARAH. You're joking.
MAX. No, I'm not.
SARAH. Why? Because of my husband? Not because of my husband, I hope. That's going a little far, I think.
MAX. No, nothing to do with your husband. It's because of my wife.

Pause.

SARAH. Your wife?
MAX. I can't deceive her any longer.
SARAH. Max . . .
MAX. I've been deceiving her for years. I can't go on with it. It's killing me.
SARAH. But darling, look –
MAX. Don't touch me.

Pause.

SARAH. What did you say?
MAX. You heard.

Pause.

SARAH. But your wife . . . knows. Doesn't she? You've told her . . . all about us. She's known all the time.
MAX. No, she doesn't know. She thinks I know a whore, that's all. Some spare-time whore, that's all. That's what she thinks.

SARAH. Yes, but be sensible . . . my love . . . she doesn't
mind, does she?

MAX. She'd mind if she knew the truth, wouldn't she?

SARAH. What truth? What are you talking about?

MAX. She'd mind if she knew that, in fact . . . I've got a full-
time mistress, two or three times a week, a woman of grace,
elegance, wit, imagination –

SARAH. Yes, yes, you have –

MAX. In an affair that's been going on for years.

SARAH. She doesn't mind, she wouldn't mind – she's happy,
she's happy.

Pause.

I wish you'd stop this rubbish, anyway.

She picks up the tea-tray and moves towards the kitchen.

You're doing your best to ruin the whole afternoon.

*She takes the tray out. She then returns, looks at MAX and
goes to him.*

Darling. You don't really think you could have what we
have with your wife, do you? I mean, my husband, for
instance, completely appreciates that I –

MAX. How does he bear it, your husband? How does he bear
it? Doesn't he smell me when he comes back in the evenings? What does he *say*? He must be mad. Now – what's
the time – half-past four – now when he's sitting in his
office, knowing what's going on here, what does he *feel*, how
does he bear it?

SARAH. Max –

MAX. How?

SARAH. He's happy for me. He appreciates the way I am. He
understands.

MAX. Perhaps I should meet him and have a word with him.

SARAH. Are you drunk?

MAX. Perhaps I should do that. After all, he's a man, like me. We're both men. You're just a bloody woman.

She slams the table.

SARAH. Stop it! What's the matter with you? What's happened to you? (*Quietly.*) Please, please, stop it. What are you doing, playing a game?

MAX. A game? I don't play games.

SARAH. Don't you? You do. Oh, you do. You do. Usually I like them.

MAX. I've played my last game.

SARAH. Why?

Slight pause.

MAX. The children.

Pause.

SARAH. What?

MAX. The children. I've got to think of the children.

SARAH. What children?

MAX. My children. My wife's children. Any minute now they'll be out of boarding school. I've got to think of them.

She sits close to him.

SARAH. I want to whisper something to you. Listen. Let me whisper to you. Mmmm? Can I? Please? It's whispering time. Earlier it was teatime, wasn't it? Wasn't it? Now it's whispering time.

Pause.

You like me to whisper to you. You like me to love you, whispering. Listen. You mustn't worry about . . . wives, husbands, things like that. It's silly. It's really silly. It's you, you now, here, here with me, here together, that's

what it is, isn't it? You whisper to me, you take tea with me,
you do that, don't you, that's what we are, that's us, love
me.

He stands up.

MAX. You're too bony.

He walks away.

That's what it is, you see. I could put up with everything
if it wasn't for that. You're too bony.

SARAH. Me? Bony? Don't be ridiculous.

MAX. I'm not.

SARAH. How can you say I'm bony?

MAX. Every move I make, your bones stick into me. I'm sick
and tired of your bones.

SARAH. What are you talking about?

MAX. I'm telling you you're too bony.

SARAH. But I'm fat! Look at me. I'm plump anyway. You
always told me I was plump.

MAX. You were plump once. You're not plump any more.

SARAH. Look at me.

He looks.

MAX. You're not plump enough. You're nowhere near plump
enough. You know what I like. I like enormous women.
Like bullocks with udders. Vast great uddered bullocks.

SARAH. You mean cows.

MAX. I don't mean cows. I mean voluminous great uddered
feminine bullocks. Once, years ago, you vaguely resembled
one.

SARAH. Oh, thanks.

MAX. But now, quite honestly, compared to my ideal . . .

He stares at her.

. . . you're skin and bone.

They stare at each other.
He puts on his jacket.

SARAH. You're having a lovely joke.
MAX. It's no joke.

He goes out. She looks after him. She turns, goes slowly
towards the bongo drum, picks it up, puts it in the cup-
board. She turns, looks at chaise a moment, walks slowly into
the bedroom, sits on the end of the bed. The lights fade.
Fade up. Early evening. Six chimes of the clock. RICHARD
comes in the front door. He is wearing his sober suit. He puts
his briefcase in cupboard, hat on hook, looks about the room,
pours a drink. SARAH *comes into the bedroom from bathroom,*
wearing a sober dress. They both stand quite still in the two
rooms for a few moments. SARAH *moves to the balcony, looks*
out, RICHARD *comes into the bedroom.*

RICHARD. Hello.

Pause.

SARAH. Hello.
RICHARD. Watching the sunset?

He picks up a bottle.

Drink?
SARAH. Not at the moment, thank you.
RICHARD. Oh, what a dreary conference. Went on all day.
Terribly fatiguing. Still, good work done, I think. Some-
thing achieved. Sorry I'm rather late. Had to have a drink
with one or two of the overseas people. Good chaps.

He sits.

How are you?
SARAH. Fine.

RICHARD. Good.

Silence.

You seem a little depressed. Anything the matter?
SARAH. No.
RICHARD. What sort of day have you had?
SARAH. Not bad.
RICHARD. Not good?

Pause.

SARAH. Fair.
RICHARD. Oh, I'm sorry.

Pause.

Good to be home, I must say. You can't imagine what a comfort it is.

Pause.

Lover come?

She does not reply.

Sarah?
SARAH. What? Sorry. I was thinking of something
RICHARD. Did your lover come?
SARAH. Oh yes. He came.
RICHARD. In good shape?
SARAH. I have a headache actually.
RICHARD. Wasn't he in good shape?

Pause.

SARAH. We all have our off days.
RICHARD. He, too? I thought the whole point of being a lover is that one didn't. I mean if I, for instance, were called upon to fulfil the function of a lover and felt disposed, shall we say, to accept the job, well, I'd as soon give it up as be found incapable of executing its proper and consistent obligation.

SARAH. You do use long words.
RICHARD. Would you prefer me to use short ones?
SARAH. No, thank you.

Pause.

RICHARD. But I am sorry you had a bad day.
SARAH. It's quite all right.
RICHARD. Perhaps things will improve.
SARAH. Perhaps.

Pause.

I hope so.

She leaves the bedroom, goes into the living-room, lights a cigarette and sits. He follows.

RICHARD. Nevertheless, I find you very beautiful.
SARAH. Thank you.
RICHARD. Yes, I find you very beautiful. I have great pride in being seen with you. When we're out to dinner, or at the theatre.
SARAH. I'm so glad.
RICHARD. Or at the Hunt Ball.
SARAH. Yes, the Hunt Ball.
RICHARD. Great pride, to walk with you as my wife on my arm. To see you smile, laugh, walk, talk, bend, be still. To hear your command of contemporary phraseology, your delicate use of the very latest idiomatic expression, so subtly employed. Yes. To feel the envy of others, their attempts to gain favour with you, by fair means or foul, your austere grace confounding them. And to know you are my wife. It's a source of a profound satisfaction to me.

Pause.

What's for dinner.
SARAH. I haven't thought.

RICHARD. Oh, why not?

SARAH. I find the thought of dinner fatiguing. I prefer not to think about it.

RICHARD. That's rather unfortunate. I'm hungry.

Slight pause.

You hardly expect me to embark on dinner after a day spent sifting matters of high finance in the City.

She laughs.

One could even suggest you were falling down on your wifely duties.

SARAH. Oh dear.

RICHARD. I must say I rather suspected this would happen, sooner or later.

Pause.

SARAH. How's your whore?

RICHARD. Splendid.

SARAH. Fatter or thinner?

RICHARD. I beg your pardon?

SARAH. Is she fatter or thinner?

RICHARD. She gets thinner every day.

SARAH. That must displease you.

RICHARD. Not at all. I'm fond of thin ladies.

SARAH. I thought the contrary.

RICHARD. Really? Why would you have thought that?

Pause.

Of course, your failure to have dinner on the table is quite consistent with the life you've been leading for some time, isn't it?

SARAH. Is it?

RICHARD. Entirely.

Slight pause.

Perhaps I'm being unkind. Am I being unkind?

SARAH (*looks at him*). I don't know.

RICHARD. Yes, I am. In the traffic jam on the bridge just now, you see, I came to a decision.

Pause.

SARAH. Oh? What?

RICHARD. That it has to stop.

SARAH. What?

RICHARD. Your debauchery.

Pause.

Your life of depravity. Your path of illegitimate lust.

SARAH. Really?

RICHARD. Yes, I've come to an irrevocable decision on that point.

She stands.

SARAH. Would you like some cold ham?

RICHARD. Do you understand me?

SARAH. Not at all. I have something cold in the fridge.

RICHARD. Too cold, I'm sure. The fact is this is my house. From today, I forbid you to entertain your lover on these premises. This applies to any time of the day. Is that understood.

SARAH. I've made a salad for you.

RICHARD. Are you drinking?

SARAH. Yes, I'll have one.

RICHARD. What are you drinking?

SARAH. You know what I drink. We've been married ten years.

RICHARD. So we have.

He pours.

It's strange, of course, that it's taken me so long to appreciate the humiliating ignominy of my position.

SARAH. I didn't take my lover ten years ago. Not quite. Not on the honeymoon.

RICHARD. That's irrelevant. The fact is I am a husband who has extended to his wife's lover open house on any afternoon of her desire. I've been too kind. Haven't I been too kind?

SARAH. But of course. You're terribly kind.

RICHARD. Perhaps you would give him my compliments, by letter if you like, and ask him to cease his visits from (*He consults calendar.*) – the twelfth inst.

Long silence.

SARAH. How can you talk like this?

Pause.

Why today . . . so suddenly?

Pause.

Mmmm?

She is close to him.

You've had a hard day . . . at the office. All those overseas people. It's so tiring. But it's silly, it's so silly, to talk like this. I'm here. For you. And you've always appreciated . . . how much these afternoons . . . mean. You've always understood.

She presses her cheek to his.

Understanding is so rare, so dear.

RICHARD. Do you think it's pleasant to know that your wife is unfaithful to you two or three times a week, with great regularity?

SARAH. Richard –

RICHARD. It's insupportable. It has become insupportable. I'm no longer disposed to put up with it.

SARAH (*to him*). Sweet . . . Richard . . . please.

RICHARD. Please what?

She stops.

Can I tell you what I suggest you do?

SARAH. What?

RICHARD. Take him out into the fields. Find a ditch. Or a slag heap. Find a rubbish dump. Mmmm? What about that?

She stands still.

Buy a canoe and find a stagnant pond. Anything. Anywhere. But not my living-room.

SARAH. I'm afraid that's not possible.

RICHARD. Why not?

SARAH. I said it's not possible.

RICHARD. But if you want your lover so much, surely that's the obvious thing to do, since his entry to this house is now barred. I'm trying to be helpful, darling, because of my love for you. You can see that. If I find him on these premises I'll kick his teeth out.

SARAH. You're mad.

He stares at her.

RICHARD. I'll kick his head in.

Pause.

SARAH. What about your own bloody whore?

RICHARD. I've paid her off.

SARAH. Have you? Why?

RICHARD. She was too bony.

Slight pause.

SARAH. But you liked . . . you said you liked . . . Richard
. . . but you love me . . .

RICHARD. Of course.

SARAH. Yes . . . you love me . . . you don't mind him . . .
you understand him . . . don't you ? . . . I mean, you know
better than I do . . . darling . . . all's well . . . all's well
. . . the evenings . . . and the afternoons . . . do you see ?
Listen, I do have dinner for you. It's ready. I wasn't serious.
It's Boeuf bourgignon. And tomorrow I'll have Chicken
Chasseur. Would you like it ?

They look at each other.

RICHARD (*softly*). Adulteress.

SARAH. You can't talk like this, it's impossible, you know you
can't. What do you think you're doing ?

*He remains looking at her for a second, then moves into the
hall.*
*He opens the hall cupboard and takes out the bongo drum.
She watches him.*
He returns.

RICHARD. What's this ? I found it some time ago. What is it ?

Pause.

What is it ?

SARAH. You shouldn't touch that.

RICHARD. But it's in my house. It belongs either to me, or to
you, or to another.

SARAH. It's nothing. I bought it in a jumble sale. It's nothing.
What do you think it is ? Put it back.

RICHARD. Nothing ? This ? A drum in my cupboard ?

SARAH. Put it back!

RICHARD. It isn't by any chance anything to do with your
illicit afternoons ?

SARAH. Not at all. Why should it?

RICHARD. It is used. This is used, isn't it? I can guess.

SARAH. You guess nothing. Give it to me.

RICHARD. How does he use it? How do you use it? Do you
play it while I'm at the office?

*She tries to take the drum. He holds on to it. They are still,
hands on the drum.*

What function does this fulfil? It's not just an ornament, I
take it? What do you do with it?

SARAH (*with quiet anguish*). You've no right to question me.
No right at all. It was our arrangement. No questions of this
kind. Please. Don't, don't. It was our arrangement.

RICHARD. I want to know.

She closes her eyes.

SARAH. Don't . . .

RICHARD. Do you both play it? Mmmmnn? Do you both
play it? Together?

She moves away swiftly, then turns, hissing.

SARAH. You stupid . . . ! (*She looks at him coolly.*) Do you think
he's the only one who comes! Do you? Do you think he's the
only one I entertain? Mmmnn? Don't be silly. I have other
visitors, other visitors, all the time, I receive all the time.
Other afternoons, all the time. When neither of you know,
neither of you. I give them strawberries in season. With
cream. Strangers, total strangers. But not to me, not while
they're here. They come to see the hollyhocks. And then they
stay for tea. Always. Always.

RICHARD. Is that so?

He moves towards her, tapping the drum gently.
*He faces her, tapping, then grasps her hand and scratches it
across the drum.*

SARAH. What are you doing?
RICHARD. Is that what you do?

> *She jerks away, to behind the table.*
> *He moves towards her, tapping.*

Like that?

> *Pause.*

What fun.

> *He scratches the drum sharply and then places it on the*
> *chair.*

Got a light?

> *Pause.*

Got a light?

> *She retreats towards the table, eventually ending behind it.*

Come on, don't be a spoilsport. Your husband won't mind,
if you give me a light. You look a little pale. Why are you
so pale? A lovely girl like you.
SARAH. Don't, don't say that!
RICHARD. You're trapped. We're alone. I've locked up.
SARAH. You mustn't do this, you mustn't do it, you mustn't!
RICHARD. He won't mind.

> *He begins to move slowly closer to the table.*

No one else knows.

> *Pause.*

No one else can hear us. No one knows we're here.

> *Pause.*

Come on. Give us a light.

Pause.

You can't get out, darling. You're trapped.

They face each other from opposite ends of the table.
She suddenly giggles.
Silence.

ARAH. I'm trapped.

Pause.

What will my husband say?

Pause.

He expects me. He's waiting. I can't get out. I'm trapped.
You've no right to treat a married woman like this. Have
you? Think, think, think of what you're doing.

She looks at him, bends and begins to crawl under the table
towards him. She emerges from under the table and kneels at
his feet, looking up. Her hand goes up his leg. He is looking
down at her.

You're very forward. You really are. Oh, you really are.
But my husband will understand. My husband does understand. Come here. Come down here. I'll explain. After all,
think of my marriage. He adores me. Come here and I'll
whisper to you. I'll whisper it. It's whispering time. Isn't
it?

She takes his hands. He sinks to his knees, with her. They
are kneeling together, close. She strokes his face.

It's a very late tea. Isn't it? But I think I like it. Aren't you
sweet? I've never seen you before after sunset. My husband's at a late-night conference. Yes, you look different.
Why are you wearing this strange suit, and this tie? You
usually wear something else, don't you? Take off your

jacket. Mmmnn? Would you like me to change? Would you like me to change my clothes? I'll change for you, darling. Shall I? Would you like that?

Silence. She is very close to him.

RICHARD. Yes.

Pause.

Change.

Pause.

Change.

Pause.

Change your clothes.

Pause.

You lovely whore.

They are still, kneeling, she leaning over him.

THE END

Night School

NIGHT SCHOOL was first presented by Associated Rediffusion Television in the version printed here on 21 July 1960 with the following cast:

ANNIE	Iris Vandeleur
WALTER	Milo O'Shea
MILLY	Jane Eccles
SALLY	Vivien Merchant
SOLTO	Martin Miller
TULLY	Bernard Spear

Directed by Joan Kemp-Welch

It was later adapted for radio by the author* and performed on the B.B.C. Third Programme on 25 September 1966 with the following cast:

ANNIE	Mary O'Farrell
WALTER	John Hollis
MILLY	Sylvia Coleridge
SALLY	Prunella Scales
SOLTO	Sydney Tafler
TULLY	Preston Lockwood
BARBARA	Barbara Mitchell
MAVIS	Carol Marsh

Directed by Guy Vaesen

* The radio version is published by Eyre Methuen in Tea Party and other plays by Harold Pinter

1. **Interior. Bedroom. Evening.** *The bedroom of a terraced house in South London. Camera pans round the room. It is neat, clean, feminine. And empty.*

2. **Interior. Living room. Evening.** WALTER *and* ANNIE *are drinking tea.*

WALTER. Beautiful tea.

ANNIE. I know it is. Look at your raincoat. It's on the floor.

WALTER. I'll hang it up. (*He crosses to pick up his coat.*) I'll take the case upstairs, eh? (*He picks up his case.*)

ANNIE. Have your tea. Go on, have your tea. Don't worry about taking the case upstairs.

He puts the case down, sits, and bites into a piece of cake. Pause.

WALTER. Lovely cake.

ANNIE. Do you like it? I've had to lay off cake. They was giving me heart-burn. Go on, have another piece.

WALTER. Ah well, the place looks marvellous.

ANNIE. I gave it a nice clean out before you came.

Pause.

Well, Wally, how did they treat you this time, eh?

WALTER. Marvellous.

ANNIE. I didn't expect you back so soon. I thought you was staying longer this time.

WALTER. No, I wasn't staying longer.

ANNIE. Milly's not been well.

WALTER. Oh? What's the matter with her?

ANNIE. She'll be down in a minute, she heard you come.

WALTER. I brought some chocolates for her.

ANNIE. I can't stand chocolates.

WALTER. I know that. That's why I didn't bring any for you.

ANNIE. You remembered eh?

WALTER. Oh yes.

ANNIE. Yes, she's been having a rest upstairs. All I do, I run up and down them stairs all day long. What about the other day, I was up doing those curtains, I came over terrible. Then she says I shouldn't have done them that way. I should have done them the other way.

WALTER. What's the matter with the curtains?

ANNIE. She says they're not hanging properly. She says I should have done them the other way. She likes them the other way. She lies up there upstairs, I'm older than she is.

ANNIE pours herself and WALTER more tea.

I went out and got that cake the minute we got your letter.

WALTER (*sighing*). Ah, you know, I've been thinking for months ... you know that? ... months ... I'll come back here ... I'll lie on my bed ... I'll see the curtains blowing by the window ... I'll have a good rest, eh?

Looking up at the ceiling.

ANNIE. There she is, she's moving herself.

WALTER. I'm going to take it easy for a few weeks.

ANNIE. You should. It's silly. You should have a rest for a few weeks.

Pause.

WALTER. How's Mr. Solto?

ANNIE. He's still the best landlord in the district. You wouldn't get a better landlord in any district.

WALTER. You're good tenants to him.

ANNIE. He's so kind. He's almost one of the family. Except he doesn't live here. As a matter of fact he hasn't been to tea for months.

WALTER. I'm going to ask him to lend me some money.

ANNIE. She's coming down.

WALTER. What's a couple of hundred to him? Nothing.

ANNIE (*whispering*). Don't say a word about the curtains.

WALTER. Eh?

ANNIE. Don't mention about the curtains. About the hanging. About what I told you about what she said about the way I hung the curtains. Don't say a word.

MILLY *enters*.

WALTER (*kissing her*). Aunty Milly.

MILLY. Did she give you a bit of cake?

WALTER. Marvellous cake.

MILLY. I told her to go and get it.

WALTER. I haven't had a bit of cake like that for nine solid months.

MILLY. It comes from down the road.

WALTER. Here you are, Aunty, here's some chocolates.

MILLY. He didn't forget that I like chocolates.

ANNIE. He didn't forget that I don't like chocolates.

MILLY. Nutty? Are they nutty?

WALTER. I picked them specially for the nuts. They were the nuttiest ones they had there.

ANNIE. Sit down, Milly. Don't stand up.

MILLY. I've been sitting down, I've been lying down, I got to stand up now and again.

WALTER. You haven't been so well, eh?

MILLY. Middling. Only middling.

ANNIE. I'm only middling as well.

MILLY. Yes, Annie's only been middling.

WALTER. Well, I'm back now, eh?

MILLY. How did they treat you this time?

WALTER. Very well. Very well.

MILLY. When you going back?

WALTER. I'm not going back.

MILLY. You ought to be ashamed of yourself, Walter, spending half your life in prison, where do you think that's going to get you?

WALTER. Half my life? What do you mean? Twice, that's all.

ANNIE. What about Borstal?

WALTER. That doesn't count.

MILLY. I wouldn't mind if you ever had a bit of luck, but what happens, every time you move yourself they take you inside.

WALTER. I've finished with all that, anyway.

MILLY. Listen, I've told you before, if you're not clever in that way you should try something else, you should open up a little business, you could get the capital from Solto, he'll lend you some money. I mean, every time you put a foot outside the door they pick you up, they put you inside, what's the good of it?

ANNIE. You going to have a jam tart, Wally?

WALTER. Sure.

(*Eats.*) Where'd you get the jam tarts?

ANNIE. Round the corner.

MILLY. Round the corner? I thought I told you to get them down the road.

ANNIE. He didn't have any down the road.

MILLIE. What are they like?

WALTER. Lovely. (*Takes another, eats. Pause.*)

MILLY. I've had to lay off tarts, haven't I Annie?

ANNIE. They was giving her heartburn.

MILLY. I had to lay off. I had to lay right off tarts, since just after Easter.

ANNIE. I bet you never had a tart in prison, Wally.

WALTER. No, I couldn't lay my hands on one.

Pause.

MILLY. Well? Have you told him?

ANNIE. Told him what?

MILLY. You haven't told him?

WALTER. Told me what?

MILLY. Eh?

ANNIE. No, I haven't.

MILLY. Why not?

ANNIE. I wasn't going to tell him.

WALTER. Tell me what?

MILLY. You said you was going to tell him.

ANNIE. I didn't have the pluck.

WALTER. What's going on here? What's all this?

Pause.

ANNIE. Have a rock cake, Wally.

WALTER. No thanks. I'm full up.

ANNIE. Go on, have a rock cake.

WALTER. No, I've had enough. Honest.

MILLY. Have a rock cake, come on.

WALTER. I can't, I'm full up!

ANNIE. I'll go and fill the pot.

MILLY. I'll go.

ANNIE. You can't go, you're not well.

MILLY. I'll go, come on, give me the pot.

ANNIE. I made the tea, why shouldn't I fill the pot?

MILLY. Can't I fill the pot for my own nephew?

WALTER. Now listen, what have you got to tell me, what's the matter? I come home from prison, I been away nine months, I come home for a bit of peace and quiet to recuperate, what's going on here?

MILLY. Well . . . we've let your room.

WALTER. You've what?

ANNIE. We've let your room.

Pause.

MILLY. We couldn't help ourselves.

Pause.

WALTER. You've done what?

ANNIE. We missed you.

MILLY. It gave us a bit of company.

ANNIE. Of course it did ...

MILLY. It gave us a helping hand ...

ANNIE. You spend half your time inside, we don't know when you're coming out ....

MILLY. We only get the pension.

ANNIE. That's all we got, we only got the pension.

MILLY She pays good money, she pays 35s. 6d. a week ...

ANNIE. She's down here every Friday morning with the rent.

MILLY. And she looks after her room, she's always dusting her room.

ANNIE. She helps me give a bit of a dust round the house.

MILLY. On the weekends ...

ANNIE. She leaves the bath as good as new ...

MILLY. And you should see what she's done to her room.

ANNIE. Oh, you should see how she's made the room.

MILLY. She's made it beautiful, she's made it really pretty ...

ANNIE. She's fitted up a lovely table lamp in there, hasn't she?

MILLY. She's always studying books ....

ANNIE. She goes out to night school three nights a week.

MILLY. She's a young girl.

ANNIE. She's a very clean girl.

MILLY. She's quiet ...

ANNIE. She's a homely girl ...

Pause.

WALTER. What's her name?

ANNIE. Sally ...

WALTER. Sally what?

MILLY. Sally Gibbs.

WALTER. How long has she been here?

MILLY. She's been here about – when did she come?

ANNIE. She came about ...

MILLY. Four months about ... she's been here ...

WALTER. What does she do for a living?

MILLY. She teaches at a school.

WALTER. A school teacher!

MILLY. Yes.

WALTER. A school teacher! In my room.

Pause.

ANNIE. Wally, you'll like her.

WALTER. She's sleeping in my room!

MILLY. What's the matter with the put-u-up? You can have the put-u-up in here.

WALTER. The put-u-up? She's sleeping in my bed.

ANNIE. She's bought a lovely coverlet, she's put it on.

WALTER. A coverlet? I could go out now. I could pick up a a coverlet as good as hers, what are you talking about coverlets for? I can't believe it, I come home after nine months in a dungeon.

ANNIE. The money's been a great help.

WALTER. Have I ever left you short of money?

MILLY. Yes!

WALTER. Well . . . not through my own fault. I've always done my best.

MILLY. And where's it got you?

WALTER. What's this, you reproaching me?

ANNIE. Your Aunt's not one to go around reproaching people, Walter.

MILLY. Live and let live, that's my motto.

ANNIE. And mine.

MILLY. It's always been my motto, you ask anyone.

WALTER. Listen, you don't understand. This is my home. I live here, I've lived in that room for years . . .

ANNIE. On and off.

WALTER. You're asking me to sleep on that put-u-up? The only person who ever slept on that put-u-up was Aunty Gracy. That's why she went to America.

MILLY. She slept in it for five years with Uncle Alf, Grace did. They never had a word of complaint.

WALTER. Uncle Alf! Honest, this has knocked me for . . . for six, I can't believe it. But I'll tell you one thing . . . I'll tell you one thing about that bed she's sleeping in.

ANNIE. What's the matter with it?

WALTER. There's nothing the matter with it. It's mine, that's all, I bought it.

ANNIE. So he did Milly.

MILLY. You? I thought I bought it.

ANNIE. That's right. You did. I remember.

WALTER. You bought it, you went out and chose it, but who gave you the money to buy it?

ANNIE. Yes, he's right. He did.

Pause.

WALTER. I mean . . . what's happened to my damn things? What's happened to my case? The one I left here?

ANNIE. Well she didn't mind us leaving your things in the cupboard, did she Milly?

WALTER. Things? That's my life's work!

Pause.

She'll have to go, that's all.

MILLY. She's not going.

WALTER. Why not?

ANNIE. She's not going to go.

MILLY. I should say not. She's staying.

Pause.

WALTER (*with fatigue*). Why can't she sleep on the put-u-up?

ANNIE. Put a lovely girl like that on the put-u-up? In the living-room?

WALTER. She's lovely, is she?

MILLY. You should see the beauty cream on her dressing-table.

WALTER. My dressing-table.

MILLY. I like a girl who looks after herself.

ANNIE. She gives herself a good going over every night.

MILLY. She's never out of the bath. Morning and night. On the nights she goes to night school, she has one before she goes out, other nights she has it just before she goes to bed.

WALTER. Well, she couldn't have it after she's gone to bed, could she?

Pause.

Night school? What kind of night school?

MILLY. She's studying foreign languages there. She's learning to speak two more languages.

ANNIE. Yes, you can smell her up and down the house.

WALTER. Smell her?

ANNIE. Lovely perfume she puts on.

MILLY. Yes, I'll say that, it's a pleasure to smell her.

WALTER. Is it?

ANNIE. There's nothing wrong with a bit of perfume.

MILLY. We're not narrow-minded over a bit of perfume.

ANNIE. She's up to date, that's all.

MILLIE. Up to the latest fashion.

ANNIE. I was, when I was a girl.

MILLY. What about me?

ANNIE. So were you. But you weren't as up to date as I was.

MILLY. I was. I didn't have anything coming over me.

Pause.

WALTER. Does she know where I've been.

ANNIE. Oh, yes.

WALTER. You told her I've been in the nick?

ANNIE. Oh, we told her, yes.

WALTER. Did you tell her why?

MILLY. Oh, no. Oh no, we didn't tell her why.

ANNIE. But it didn't worry her, did it, Milly? I mean she was very interested. Oh, she was terribly interested.

> WALTER *looks up at the ceiling slowly.*

WALTER. She was, was she?

3. Interior. Sally's bedroom. Evening. SALLY's *legs. She sits, kicks off her shoes, picks up a small pile of exercise books, puts them on her knee and starts making corrections. We do not see her face.*

4. Interior. Living room. Evening. WALTER *stands abruptly, slamming the table.*

WALTER. Where am I going to put my case?

ANNIE. You can put it in the hall.

WALTER. The hall? That means I'll have to keep running out to the hall whenever I want anything.

> *Pause.*

I can't live in these conditions for long. I'm used to something better. I'm used to privacy. I could have her walking in here any time of the day or night. This is the living room. I don't want to share my meals with a stranger.

ANNIE. She only has bed and breakfast. I take it up to her room.

WALTER. What does she have?

ANNIE. She has a nice piece of bacon with a poached egg, and she enjoys every minute of it.

WALTER. For 35s. 6d. a week. They're charging £3 10s. everywhere up and down the country. She's doing you. She's got hot and cold running water, every comfort, breakfast in a first class bed. She's taking you for a ride.

ANNIE. No, she's not.

Pause.

WALTER. I left something in my room. I'm going to get it.

5. Interior. Hall and stairway. Evening. *He goes out and up the stairs. The bathroom door opens and* SALLY *comes out. Descends stairs half way down.*

They meet.

SALLY (*humming*). Mr. Street?

WALTER. Yes?

SALLY. I'm so pleased to meet you. I've heard so much about you.

WALTER. Oh, yes?

Pause.

I ... er ...

SALLY. Your aunts are charming people.

WALTER. Mmmmm.

Pause.

SALLY. Are you glad to be back?

WALTER. I've left something in my room. I've got to get it.

SALLY. Oh, well, we'll meet again. Bye-bye.

She goes to her room. He follows.

WALTER. Could I just ...?

SALLY. What?

WALTER. Come in.

SALLY. Come in? But ... well, yes ... do ... if you want to.

They go in.

6. Interior. Sally's bedroom. Evening. WALTER *follows her in, shutting the door behind him*

SALLY. I'm sorry. (*She goes to the dressing-table and tidies it.*) Everything's all over the place. I'm at school all day. I don't have much time to tidy up.

Pause.

I believe I'm teaching at the school you went to. In the infants.

WALTER. Round the corner? Yes, I went there.

SALLY. You wouldn't believe all the things I've heard about you. You're the apple of your aunts' eyes.

WALTER. So are you.

Pause.

SALLY. I'm happy here. I get on very well with them.

WALTER. Look . . . I've got to get something in here.

SALLY. In here? I thought you said you'd left something in your room.

WALTER. This is my room.

Pause.

SALLY. This?

WALTER. You've taken my room.

SALLY. Have I? I never . . . realised that. Nobody ever told me that. I'm terribly sorry. Do you want it back?

WALTER. I wouldn't mind.

SALLY. Oh dear . . . this is . . . awkward . . . I must say I'm very comfortable here . . . I mean where else could I sleep?

WALTER. There's a put-u-up downstairs.

SALLY. Oh, I don't trust those things, do you? I mean, this is such a lovely bed.

WALTER. I know it is. It's mine.

SALLY. You mean I'm sleeping in your bed?

WALTER. Yes.

SALLY. Oh.

Pause.

WALTER. I've got something in here I want to get.

SALLY. Well . . . carry on.

WALTER. It's in a rather private place.

SALLY. Do you want me to go out?

WALTER. Yes, if you don't mind.

SALLY. Go out of the room, you mean?

WALTER. It'll only take a minute.

SALLY. What are you looking for?

WALTER. It's a private matter.

SALLY. Is it a gun?

Pause.

Can't I turn my back?

WALTER. Two minutes. That's all I want.

SALLY. All right. Two minutes.

She leaves the room.

WALTER goes to a cupboard, opens it. In it are SALLY's clothes, books, knick-knacks. He locates a compartment at the back of the cupboard, opens it, takes out a large envelope, closes the compartment, pushes some cardboard boxes against the compartment. The lid of one of the boxes slides off. His eye catches a photograph. He picks it up, looks at it. It is SALLY, her hair up, sitting at a table with two men. She is wearing a tight, low-cut blouse. One of the men we will later recognize as Tully. In the photograph, her right hand is on one of the men's faces. Her left holds a glass. WALTER puts the photograph in his envelope and the envelope into his jacket pocket. He closes the cupboard door, goes to the room door, opens it. SALLY is standing on the landing. She comes in.

SALLY. Find it?

WALTER. Yes, thank you.

He goes to the door, turns.

What do you teach, ballet?

SALLY. Ballet? No. What a funny question.

WALTER. Not funny. Lots of women teach ballet.

SALLY. I don't dance.

Pause.

WALTER. I'm sorry I disturbed your . . . evening.

SALLY. That's all right.

WALTER. Goodnight.

SALLY. Goodnight.

He goes. SALLY *closes the door. She goes to the dressing-table, sits and looks at herself in the mirror.*

7. Interior. Living room. Afternoon.

ANNIE. Have another piece of lemon meringue, Mr. Solto.

SOLTO. With pleasure.

ANNIE. You'll like it.

SOLTO. They wanted three hundred and fifty-five pounds income tax off me the other day. My word of honour. I said to them you must be mad! What are you trying to do, bring me to an early death? Buy me a cheap spade I'll get up first thing in the morning before breakfast and dig my own grave. Three hundred and fifty-five nicker eh? I said to them I said, show me it, I said show me it down in black and white, show me where I've earned — must be round about a thousand pound, you ask me for all that. It's an estimate, they said, we've estimated your earnings. An estimate? Who did your *estimate*? A blind man with double vision? I'm an old age pensioner. I'm in receipt of three pound a week, find me something to estimate! What do you say, Walter?

WALTER. They're all villains, the lot of them.

ANNIE. They don't care for the old.

MILLY. Still, you've still got plenty of energy left in you, Mr. Solto.

SOLTO. Plenty of what?

MILLY. Energy.

SOLTO. Energy? You should have seen me in the outback in Australia. I was the man who opened up the Northern Territory for them out there.

MILLY. It's a wonder you never got married, Mr. Solto.

SOLTO. I've always been a lone wolf. The first time I was seduced, I said to myself, Solto, watch your step, mind how you go, go so far but no further. If they want to seduce you, let them seduce you, but marry them? Out of the question.

WALTER. Where was that, in Australia or Greece?

SOLTO. Australia.

WALTER. How did you get to Australia from Greece?

SOLTO. By sea. How do you think? I worked my passage. And what a trip. I was only a pubescent. I killed a man with my own hands, a six foot ten lascar from Madagascar.

ANNIE. From Madagascar.

SOLTO. Sure. A lascar.

MILLY. Alaska?

SOLTO. Madagascar!

Pause.

WALTER. It's happened before.

SOLTO. And it'll happen again.

MILLY. Have a chocolate eclair, Mr. Solto.

SOLTO. What a lovely idea.

WALTER. How's the scrap business, Mr. Solto?

SOLTO. Ssshh! That's the same question the tax inspector

asked me. I told him I retired years ago. He says to me why don't you fill out your income tax returns? Why don't you fill out all the forms we send you? I said, I got no income tax to declare, that's why. You're the only man in the district who won't fill out his forms, he says, you want to go to prison? Prison, I said, a man like me, a clean living old man like me, a man who discovered Don Bradman, it's a national disgrace! Fill out your forms, he says, there'll be no trouble. Listen! I said, if you want me to fill out those forms, if you want me to go through all that clerical work, all right, pay me a small sum, pay me for my trouble. Pay me to do it. Otherwise, fill them out yourself, leave me alone. Three hundred and fifty-five nicker? They got a fat chance.

ANNIE. A good wife wouldn't have done you no harm. She'd fill out your forms – for you.

SOLTO. That's what I'm afraid of.

MILLY. Have a custard tart, Mr. Solto.

ANNIE. He's still got a good appetite.

SOLTO. I've been saving it up since I last come here.

WALTER. Why, when were you last here, Mr. Solto?

MILLY. It was just after you went inside.

SOLTO. I brought round some daffodils.

ANNIE. Nine months ago, he remembers.

SOLTO. How're they doing?

ANNIE. What?

SOLTO. The daffodils.

ANNIE. Oh, they died.

SOLTO. Go on! (*Eats.*)

WALTER. So you don't know about the lodger?

SOLTO. Lodger?

WALTER. Yes, we've got a lodger now.

MILLY. She's a school teacher.

SOLTO. A school teacher eh? Where does she sleep? On the put-u-up?

WALTER. My aunts gave her my room.

MILLY. Come on Annie help me clear the table.

The old ladies start to clear the table.

SOLTO. The lady who first seduced me, in Australia – she kicked her own husband out and gave me his room. I bumped into him years later making a speech at Marble Arch. It wasn't a bad speech it so happens.

MILLY (*stacking plates*). Why don't you lend Wally a few pound, Mr. Solto?

SOLTO. Me?

ANNIE. Yes, why don't you?

MILLY. You could help to set him up.

SOLTO. Why don't you go to the Prisoners' Help Society? They'll give you a loan. I mean you've done two stretches, you must have a few good references.

WALTER. You wouldn't miss two hundred quid.

SOLTO. Two hundred here, three fifty-five there – do me a favour!

MILLY. You can't take it with you, Mr. Solto.

WALTER. He wants to be the richest man in the cemetery.

ANNIE. It won't do you much good where you're going, Mr. Solto.

SOLTO. Who's going anywhere?

MILLY. Come on, Annabel.

ANNIE. There's one rock cake left, Mr. Solto.

SOLTO. I'll tell you what, Annie. Keep the rock cake.

MILLY. Annabel.

ANNIE *and* MILLY *go out with the plates.*

SOLTO. I wish I could give you a helping hand, Wally. Honest. But things are very tight. I had six cross doubles the other day. Three came home. Number four developed rheumatism at the last hurdle. I went without food for two days.

WALTER. I could do with a lift up. I'm thinking of going straight.

SOLTO. Why? You getting tired of a life of crime?

WALTER. I'm not good enough. I get caught too many times. I'm not clever enough.

SOLTO. You're still on the post office books?

WALTER. Yes.

SOLTO. It's a mug's game. I've told you before. If you want to be a forger, you've got to have a gift. A real gift. It's got to come from the heart.

WALTER. I'm not a good enough forger.

SOLTO. You're a terrible forger.

WALTER. That's why I'm always getting caught.

SOLTO. I'm a better forger than you any day. And I don't forge.

WALTER. I haven't got the gift.

SOLTO. A forger's got to love his work. You don't love your work, that's your trouble, Walter.

WALTER. If you lent me two hundred quid I could go straight.

SOLTO. I'm an old age pensioner, Wally. What are you talking about?

WALTER. If only I could get my room back! I could get settled in, I could think about things!

SOLTO. Why, who's this school teacher, then? What's the game?

WALTER (*casually*). Listen, I want to show you something.

SOLTO. What?

WALTER. This photo.

SOLTO. Who's this?

WALTER. A girl ... I want to find.

SOLTO. Who is she?

WALTER. That's what I want to find out.

SOLTO. We were just talking about forging, about your room, about the school teacher. What's this got to do with it?

WALTER. This is a club isn't it, in the photo?

SOLTO. Sure.

WALTER. And the girl's a hostess, isn't she?

SOLTO. Sure.

WALTER. Can you locate her?

SOLTO. Me?

Pause.

WALTER. Do you know any of these men – these men with her?

SOLTO. O-oh, one of them . . . looks familiar.

WALTER. Find that girl for me. It's important. As a favour. You're the only man I know who could find her. You know these clubs.

SOLTO. Do you know the girl?

Pause.

WALTER. No.

SOLTO. Well, where'd you get hold of the photo?

WALTER. I got hold of it.

SOLTO. What have you done? Fallen in love with a photo?

WALTER. Sure. That's right.

SOLTO. Yes . . . A very attractive girl. A lovely girl. All right Wally. I'll try and find her for you.

The front door slams. Footsteps up the stairs.

SOLTO. Who's that?

WALTER. That's our lodger. The school teacher.

8. Interior. Sally's bedroom. Night. SALLY *is lying on the bed, smoking, looking up at the ceiling.*

9. Interior. Living room. Night. WALTER *is sitting at the table with a pile of post-office savings books. He is carefully copying signatures onto a sheet of paper. He stops, leans back, looks up at the ceiling.*

10. Interior. Aunts' bedroom. Night. *Two single beds.* MILLY *is in bed.* ANNIE *enters with a tray on which is a glass of milk on a saucer, one doughnut and a plate of anchovies.*

MILLY. I don't want the milk hot, I want it cold.

ANNIE. It is cold.

MILLY. I thought you warmed it up.

ANNIE. I did. The time I got up here, it's gone cold.

MILLY. You should have kept it in the pan. If you'd brought it up in the pan it would have still been hot.

ANNIE. I thought you said you didn't want it hot.

MILLY. I don't want it hot.

ANNIE. Well, that's why I'm saying it's cold.

MILLY. I know that. But say if I had wanted it hot. That's all I'm saying. (*She sips the milk.*) It could be colder.

ANNIE. Do you want a piece of anchovy or a doughnut?

MILLY. I'll have the anchovy. What are you going to have?

ANNIE. I'm going downstairs to have a doughnut.

MILLY. You can have this one.

ANNIE. No, I've got one downstairs. You can have it after the anchovy.

MILLY. Why don't you have the anchovy?

ANNIE. You know what I wouldn't mind? I wouldn't mind a few pilchards.

MILLY. Herring. A nice bit of herring, that's what I could do with.

ANNIE. A few pilchards with a drop of vinegar. And a plate of chocolate mousse to go after it.

MILLY. Chocolate mousse?

ANNIE. Don't you remember when we had chocolate mousse at Clacton?

MILLY. Chocolate mousse wouldn't go with herrings.

ANNIE. I'm not having herrings. I'm having pilchards.

Noise of steps upstairs.

Listen.

ANNIE *turns the door-handle, listens.*
WALTER *knocks on* SALLY's *door.*

SALLY. Yes?
WALTER. It's me.
SALLY. Just a moment. Come in.

The door opens.

WALTER. How are you?
SALLY. I'm fine.

The door closes.

ANNIE. He's in.
MILLY. What do you mean, he's in?
ANNIE. He's gone in.
MILLY. Gone in where, Annie?
ANNIE. Into her room.
MILLY. His room.
ANNIE. His room.
MILLY. He's gone in?
ANNIE. Yes.
MILLY. Is she in there?
ANNIE. Yes.
MILLY. So he's in there with her.
ANNIE. Yes.
MILLY. Go out and have a listen.

11. Interior. Upstairs landing. Night. ANNIE *comes out of her bedroom and goes down the landing to* SALLY'*s door where she stops.*

12. Interior. Sally's bedroom. Night.

WALTER. Looking very nice in here.
SALLY. Yes it is, isn't it?
WALTER. Let's have some of this. I've brought it for you.
SALLY. What is it?

WALTER. Brandy.

SALLY. What's this in aid of?

WALTER. Well, I thought we might as well get to know each other, both living in the same house.

SALLY. Yes, why not?

WALTER. Do you drink?

SALLY. Oh, not really.

WALTER. Just one or two now and again, eh?

SALLY. Very occasionally.

WALTER. But you'll have a drop of this?

SALLY. Just a drop ... Glasses ...

WALTER. I've got them.

SALLY. All prepared, eh?

He opens the bottle and pours.

WALTER. Cheers.

SALLY. Good health.

WALTER. I wanted to say ... I was a bit rude yesterday, I wanted to apologise.

SALLY. You weren't rude.

WALTER. It'll just take a bit of getting used to, that's all, you having my room.

SALLY. Well, look, I've been thinking ... perhaps we could share the room – in – in a kind of way.

WALTER. Share it?

SALLY. I mean, you could use it when I'm not here, or something.

WALTER. Oh, I don't know about that.

SALLY. It'd be quite easy. I'm at school all day.

WALTER. What about the evenings?

SALLY. Well, I'm out three nights a week, you see.

WALTER. Where do you go?

SALLY. Oh, night school. I'm studying languages. Then I usually go on with a girl friend of mine, a history teacher, to listen to some music.

WALTER. What kind of music?

SALLY. Mozart, Brahms. That kind of stuff.

WALTER. Oh, all that kind of stuff.

SALLY. Yes.

Pause.

WALTER. Well, it's cosy in here. Have another one.

SALLY. Oh, I . . .

WALTER (*pouring*). Just one.

SALLY. Thanks. Cheers.

Pause.

WALTER. I've never been in this room with a lady before.

SALLY. Oh.

WALTER. The boys used to come here though. This is where we used to plan our armed robberies.

SALLY. Really?

WALTER. My aunts never told you why I've been inside, have they?

SALLY. No.

WALTER. Well, what it is, you see. I'm a gunman.

SALLY. Oh.

WALTER. Ever met a gunman before?

SALLY. I don't think so.

WALTER. It's not a bad life, all things considered. Plenty of time off. You know, holidays with pay, you could say. No, there's plenty of worse occupations. You're not frightened of me now you know I'm a gunman, are you?

SALLY. No, I think you're charming.

WALTER. Oh, you're right there. That's why I got on so well in prison, you see. Charm. You know what I was doing in there, I was running the prison library. I was the best librarian they ever had. The day I left the Governor gave me a personal send-off. Saw me all the way to the gate. He told me business at the library had shot up out of all recognition since I'd been in charge.

SALLY. What a wonderful compliment.

WALTER (*pouring more drink*). He told me that if I'd consider giving up armed robbery, he'd recommend me for a job in the British Museum. Looking after rare manuscripts. You know, writing my opinion of them.

SALLY. I should think that's quite a skilled job.

WALTER. Cheers. Skilled? Well, funny enough, I've had a good bit to do with rare manuscripts in my time. I used to know a bloke who ran a business digging them up.

SALLY. Digging what up?

WALTER. Rare manuscripts. Out of tombs. I used to give him a helping hand when I was on the loose. Very well paid it was too. You see, they were nearly always attached to a corpse, these manuscripts, you had to lift up the pelvis bone with a pair of tweezers. Big tweezers. Can't leave finger-prints on a corpse, you see. Canon law. The biggest shock I ever had was when a skeleton collapsed on top of me and nearly bit my ear off. I had a funny feeling at that moment. I thought I was the skeleton and he was my long-lost uncle come to kiss me goodnight. You've never been inside a grave, I suppose. I can recommend it, honest, I mean if you want to taste everything life has to offer.

SALLY. Well, I'll be inside one, one day.

WALTER. Oh, I don't know. You might be cremated, or drowned at sea, mightn't you?

13. Interior. Upstairs landing. Night. ANNIE *creeps back down the landing to the* AUNTS' *room and goes back in.*

14. Interior. Aunts' room. Night. ANNIE *starts to get back into bed.*

MILLY. Did you listen?

ANNIE. Yes.

MILLY. Well?

ANNIE. I heard them talking.

MILLY. What were they saying?

ANNIE. Don't ask me.

MILLY. Go to the door again. Listen properly.

ANNIE. Why don't you go?

MILLY. I'm in bed.

ANNIE. So am I.

MILLY. But I've been in bed longer than you.

ANNIE *mutters and grumbles to herself but gets out of bed and goes back out onto the landing.*

15. Interior. Upstairs landing. Night. ANNIE *emerges from the* AUNTS' *bedroom and goes back to listen at* SALLY's *door.*

16. Interior. Sally's bedroom. Night.

WALTER. Yes, it's not a bad drop of brandy, this.

SALLY. Yes, it's very warming.

WALTER. You're a Northerner?

SALLY. That's clever of you. I thought I'd . . .

WALTER. I can tell the accent.

SALLY. I thought I'd lost it . . .

WALTER. There's something in your eyes too. You only find it in Lancashire girls.

SALLY. Really? What?

WALTER (*moving closer*). You seem a bit uncomfortable with me. Why's that?

SALLY. I'm not uncomfortable.

WALTER. Why's that then? You seem a bit uneasy.

SALLY. I'm not.

WALTER. Let's fill you up eh? I mean you were different yesterday. You were on top of yourself yesterday.

SALLY. It's you who were different. You're different today.

WALTER. You don't want to worry about me being an armed robber. They call me the gentle gunman.

SALLY. I'm not worried.

Pause.

WALTER. My aunties think you're marvellous. I think they've got us in mind for the marriage stakes.

SALLY. What?

WALTER. Yes, I think they think they've found me a wife.

SALLY. How funny.

WALTER. They've roped you in to take part in a wedding. They've forgotten one thing though.

SALLY. What's that?

WALTER. I'm married. As a matter of fact I'm married to three women. I'm a triple bigamist. Do you believe me?

SALLY. I think you're in a very strange mood.

WALTER. It's the look in your eyes that's brought it on.

SALLY. You haven't got such bad eyes yourself.

WALTER. Your eyes, they're Northern eyes. They're full of soot.

SALLY. Thank you.

WALTER (*pouring*). Top it up. Come on.

SALLY. To our eyes.

WALTER. I thought you didn't drink. You can knock it back all right. Keep in practice in school I suppose. In the milk break. Keeps you in trim for netball. Or at that night school, eh? I bet you enjoy yourself there. Come on. Tell me what you get up to at that night school.

17. Interior. Upstairs landing. Night. ANNIE *yawns slightly and pads back to her own room.*

18. Interior. Aunts' bedroom. Night. ANNIE *gets back into bed again.*

ANNIE. Still talking.

MILLY. What are they talking about? (*Sleepily.*)

ANNIE. I can't make it out.

MILLY. I should have gone. You're deaf as a post.

They settle in bed.

ANNIE. The doughnut's given me heartburn. (*Faintly.*) Goodnight.

MILLY *snores briefly.*

19. Interior. Sally's bedroom. Night.

SALLY. I lead a quiet life, a very quiet life. I don't mix with people.

WALTER. Except me. You're mixing with me.

SALLY. I don't have any kind of social life.

WALTER. I'll have to take you round a few of the clubs I know, show you the sights.

SALLY. No, I don't like that.

WALTER. What do you like?

Pause.

SALLY. Lying here . . . by myself . . .

WALTER. On my bed.

SALLY. Yes.

WALTER. Doing what?

SALLY. Thinking.

WALTER. Think about me last night?

SALLY. You?

WALTER. This offer to share your room. I might consider it.

Pause.

I bet you're thinking about me now.

Pause.

SALLY. Why should I be?

WALTER. I'm thinking about you.

Pause.

I don't know why I made such a fuss about this room. It's just an ordinary room, there's nothing to it. I mean if you weren't here. If you weren't in it, there'd be nothing to it.

Pause.

Why don't you stay in it? It's not true that I'm married. I just said that. I'm not attached. To tell you the truth ... to tell you the truth, I'm still looking for Miss Right.

SALLY. I think I should move away from here.

WALTER. Where would you go?

Pause.

SALLY. Anywhere.

WALTER. Would you go to the seaside? I could come with you. We could do a bit of fishing ... on the Pier. Yes, we could go together. Or, on the other hand, we could stay here. We could stay where we are.

SALLY. Could we?

WALTER. Sit down.

SALLY. What?

WALTER. Sit down. (*Pause.*) Cross your legs.

SALLY. Mmmmm?

WALTER. Cross your legs.

Pause.

Uncross them.

Pause.

Stand up.

Pause.

Turn round.

Pause.

Stop.

Pause.

Sit down.

Pause.

Cross your legs.

Pause.

Uncross your legs.

Silence.

20. Interior. Night club. Night. *It is about 9 p.m. The place is still empty. A trio plays softly – piano, double bass, clarinet.* SOLTO *is drinking with* TULLY.

TULLY. No, I tell you, it must be . . . wait a minute, must be round about ten years. The last time was when I was down at Richmond.

SOLTO. Yes, the Donkey Club.

TULLY. The Donkey, sure. I left there three years ago.

SOLTO. How long you been here then? I haven't been down here for about three years.

TULLY. You must have just missed me. I come here three years ago, that's exactly when I come here. (*Calls.*) Charley!

TULLY *clicks fingers for* WAITER.

SOLTO. It was a real dive before then, I can tell you.

WAITER. Same again, Mr. Tully?

TULLY. Same again. Dive – course it was a dive. They asked me to come here and give it – you know – a bit of class, about three years ago. I gave the boot to about a dozen lowlives from the start, you know, I made my position clear.

SOLTO. Didn't they give you no trouble?

TULLY. With me? Listen, they know if they want to start making trouble, they picked the right customer. Don't you remember me at Blackheath?

SOLTO. You're going back a bit.

TULLY. I'm going back a few years before the war.

SOLTO. You're going back to when the game was good.

TULLY. What about you at Blackheath?

SOLTO. Blackheath. It's another story when you start talking about Blackheath.

TULLY. Thanks Charley. Here you are Ambrose. Cheers.

Pause.

No, you can see it's not a dive no more. I got the place moving, I mean, we got a band up there – well, I say a band – a piano and a double bass, clarinet, but they're very good boys, they're good boys. We got a very nice clientèle come in here. You know you get a lot of musicians . . . er . . . musicians coming down here. They make up a very nice clientèle. Of course, you get a certain amount of business executives. I mean, high class people. I was talking to a few of them only the other night. They come over from Hampton Court, they come, from Twickenham, from Datchet.

SOLTO. All the way from Datchet?

TULLY. Sure, they get in the car, how long's it taken them? They come here for a bit of relaxation. I mean we got a two o'clock licence. We got four resident birds. What made you come down here all of a sudden?

SOLTO. Ah, just one of them funny things, Cyril. I heard of a little bird.

TULLY. What, one of the birds here?

SOLTO. Still sharp, eh, Cyril?

TULLY. You heard about the quality we got here, eh? We got some high class dolls down here, don't worry. It's not trash. They come all the way from finishing school.

21. Interior. Girls' dressing-room. Night. *The girls –* SALLY, BARBARA, MAVIS, CAROL *– are changing ready for the evening.*

BARBARA. What did he say then?

SALLY. Come over with me one Sunday, he says, come over and have Sunday dinner, meet the wife. Why, I said, what are you going to introduce me as, your sister? No, he says, she's very broadminded, my wife, she'll be delighted to meet you.

MAVIS. Oh yes, I've heard of that kind of thing before.

SALLY. Yes, that's what I said. Oh yes, I said, I've heard of that kind of thing before. Go on, get off out of it, I said, buzz off before I call a copper.

CAROL. Which was he, the one with the big nose?

SALLY. Yes.

The MANAGER *comes in.*

MANAGER. Come on girls, move yourselves, we're ready for the off.

BARBARA. Who asked you to come into the ladies' room?

MANAGER. Don't give me no lip. Get your skates on. (*To* SALLY.) Cyril wants you at the table right away. (MANAGER *goes.*)

SALLY. I'll kick him in the middle of his paraphernalia one of these days.

BARBARA. Go on, what happened then?

SALLY. Why don't you come on the river with me one of these days, he says. I'll take you for a ride in a punt.

CAROL. In a what?

MAVIS. A punt.

CAROL. What's a punt?

SALLY. I said to him, in a punt with you? You must be mad. You won't get me in no punt.

BARBARA. I thought you said he attracted you.

SALLY. Oh, he did to start off, that's all. I thought he wasn't bad. But, you know, he came from Hungary. He'd got a lot of Hungarian habits, they didn't go down very well with me.

MANAGER *comes back.*

MANAGER. Come on, come on, I don't want to tell you again. Where do you think you are, on Brighton front? (*To* SALLY:) Cyril wants you at his table

SALLY. I'll cut his ears off one of these days.

22. Interior. Night club. Night.

SOLTO. So I thought to myself Tully, Big Johnny Bolsom. She must be all right.

TULLY. Sure she's all right.

SOLTO. So I thought I'd follow it up.

TULLY. You couldn't have done better. (SALLY *appears.*) Here she is, here she is, come on darling. This an old friend of mine, Ambrose Solto.

SALLY *sits at the table.*

SOLTO. How do you do?

SALLY. How do you do?

TULLY. Sit down, Ambrose. I want you to meet this girl, Ambrose. This is the cleverest girl we got here. She speaks three languages.

SOLTO. What languages?

TULLY. Tell him.

SALLY. Well, English for a start.

SOLTO. She's witty too eh?

TULLY. Witty? She's my favourite girl.

SALLY. Oh, I'm not.

SOLTO. Aren't you going to tell me your name?

SALLY. Katina.

SOLTO. Katina, what a coincidence. My childhood sweetheart was called Katina.

TULLY. No. Go on!

SALLY. Really Mr. Solto?

SOLTO. Yes, when I was a little boy, when I was a little boy in Athens. That's when it was.

23. Interior. Living room. Night.

WALTER. I just took the train down to Southend, that's all.

ANNIE. Southend? What for?

WALTER. I felt like having a look at the seaside. It wasn't bad down there. I rolled around that's all. Smelt the old sea, that's all.

Pause.

ANNIE. You've got a secret.

WALTER. Have I?

ANNIE. Oh, come on, Wally, what do you think of her? She's nice, isn't she?

WALTER. Who, the girl upstairs? Yes, she's a very nice girl.

ANNIE. You like her, eh?

WALTER. Who?

ANNIE. Don't you?

WALTER. What, the one that lives upstairs?

ANNIE. All larking aside.

WALTER. Well ... all larking aside ... without any larking ... I'd say she was all right.

ANNIE. You didn't like her though the first going off, did you?

WALTER. Ah well, the first going off ... ain't anything like ... the second going off, is it? What I mean to say ... is that the second going off ... often turns out to be very different ... from what you thought it was going to be ... on the first going off. If you see what I'm saying.

ANNIE. Hasn't she made the room lovely, eh?

WALTER. Very snazzy.

ANNIE. She's made it really feminine, hasn't she?

WALTER. Oh . . . without a shadow of a doubt.

24. Interior. Night club. Night. *It is later. People are dancing.* SOLTO *and* SALLY *are dancing.*

SOLTO. What do you think of that?

SALLY. You've got real rhythm, Mr. Solto. It's a pleasure.

SOLTO. I've always had rhythm. Take it from me. I was born with rhythm. My big toe can dance a polka by himself. My word of honour. My sweetheart and me, we used to dance by the sea at night, with the waves coming in. You ever done that?

SALLY. No. Never. Let's have a drink.

They go back to the table.

TULLY. How you getting on, you two?

SOLTO. Marvellous.

SALLY. Lovely.

SOLTO. See us on the floor?

TULLY. What were you doing on the floor?

SALLY. Dancing!

SOLTO. You should have seen him at Blackheath. Go on, off you go, Cyril, we're talking about philosophy here.

TULLY. Mind how you go. (*Goes.*)

SOLTO. I was going to say something to you.

SALLY. What?

SOLTO. I own a private beach. On the south coast. It's all my own. A little beach hut. Well, not so little. It's big. It's not a hut either. It's a bit bigger than a hut. It's got Indian carpets, it's got the front side full of windows looking out to the sea it's got central heating, and the waves . . . the waves come right up to the front step. You can lie on a divan and watch them come closer and closer. How would you like to lie there in the moonlight, eh, and watch the waves come closer and closer?

SALLY. Sounds ... very nice.

SOLTO. Next weekend we'll go down, eh?

SALLY. Well, I ...

SOLTO. No excuses! I'll barbecue a boar on the beach, my word of honour.

SALLY. Where you going to get the boar?

SOLTO. Specially from France, where else? Listen. You want to know a little secret, I came down here specifically to look for you.

SALLY. What do you mean?

SOLTO. I got hold of this photo of you, see? And I saw you were sitting with Tully. So here I am.

SALLY. Where'd you get the photo?

SOLTO. That I'm not supposed to tell you. You see, what I was doing, I was looking for you for a pal of mine.

SALLY. A pal? ... Who?

SOLTO. Don't worry about it. I'm not going to tell him where he can find you. No. I wouldn't let a man like that get hold of a lovely girl like you.

SALLY. What's his name?

SOLTO. He's a man called Wally. Wally Street. He's always in and out of the nick. He's a forger, a petty thief, does post office books. You know him?

SALLY. No.

SOLTO. Funny ... I don't know what he ... anyway, forget all about it. But I'll give him his due. If it wasn't for him showing me this photo where would I be, eh? And where would you be?

SALLY. Yes. Where would I be?

25. Interior. Living room. Late night. WALTER *alone. Sound of a taxi. A ring at the bell.*

26. Interior. Hall. Late night. WALTER *crosses to the front door. He opens it.* SOLTO *is there.*

SOLTO. Hallo, Wally, I'll come in a minute. I've got a cab outside.

27. Interior. Living room. Late night. WALTER *and* SOLTO *come in from the hall.*

WALTER. What's up? Have you found the girl?
SOLTO. The girl? What girl?
WALTER. The girl. That photo I gave you. You know.
SOLTO. Oh the girl! You mean the girl I was trying to . . .
WALTER. Yes, I thought that might be why you've come round.
SOLTO. You're dead right. That's exactly why I've come round.
WALTER. That's what I thought.
SOLTO. And you weren't wrong.

Pause.

WALTER. Well. Where is she?
SOLTO. That's what I wanted to tell you. I can't find her.
WALTER. You can't find her?
SOLTO. Not a smell. That's exactly what I came round to tell you.
WALTER. Not a smell, eh.
SOLTO. Not a whiff.
WALTER. I thought you were on her track.
SOLTO. There's no track. I been everywhere. The Madrigal. The Whip Room. The Gamut. Pedro's. Nobody knew the face. Wait a minute, Pedro said he might have seen her once round a few back doubles in Madrid. She been to Madrid?

WALTER. How would I know? I've never met her.

SOLTO. I thought you had.

WALTER. Didn't you locate that club?

SOLTO. What club?

WALTER. In the photo.

SOLTO. No. What I thought, the best thing to do would be to get hold of the photographer you see. So I paid him a call.

WALTER. What did he say?

SOLTO. He wasn't there. He's gone to Canada for a conference.

WALTER. What kind of conference?

SOLTO. A dental conference. He's going to be a dentist.

WALTER. Why'd he give up photography?

SOLTO. He had a change of heart. You know how it is. He gave me a cup of coffee, told me his life story.

WALTER. Who did?

SOLTO. His brother. The chiropodist. He's in dead trouble that boy, he can't meet his overheads.

WALTER. Look here, Mr. Solto, if I were you I'd give up the whole thing.

SOLTO. You want my opinion? I think the photo's a fake. There's no such club. There's no girl. They don't exist.

WALTER. That's exactly what I think.

Pause.

SOLTO. You do?

WALTER. Exactly.

SOLTO. Who knows? You may be right.

WALTER. That photo. It's a fake. You'll never find her.

SOLTO. How can it be a fake? I thought you knew her.

WALTER. I never said I knew her. I've never met her.

SOLTO. But that's what I'm saying. There's no one to know. You've never seen her. I've never seen her. There's no one to see.

WALTER. She doesn't exist.

Pause.

SOLTO. All the same, look, the girl's there. That's the photo of someone.

WALTER. No one I know.

Pause.

SOLTO. Take my tip, Wally, wipe the whole business from your head, wipe it clean out of your mind.

WALTER. That's what I think you'd better do, Mr. Solto.

The front door closes. Footsteps go upstairs.

SOLTO. What's that?

WALTER. That's the school teacher.

SOLTO. That's your mark. Someone with an education. She keeps nice hours for a schoolteacher. Where's she been, night school?

28. **Interior. Upstairs landing. Late night.** *Outside* SALLY's *room. We hear the front door close and the taxi drive off.* WALTER *comes up the stairs, knocks on* SALLY's *door.*

WALTER. Are you there?

He tries the door. It's locked.

Are you in there? I want to speak to you. Let me in a minute. Will you let me in a minute? What's up with you? What the hell's up with you? Let me in. I want to speak to you.

29. **Interior. Hall and stairs. Morning.** ANNIE *is in the* hall. MILLY, *coming downstairs, is stopped before reaching ground level.*

ANNIE. She's gone.

MILLY. Gone?

ANNIE. Here's a note.

MILLY. Where's she gone.

ANNIE. She left a note. Look, to the Misses Billet.

MILLY. What does it say?

ANNIE. Dear Misses Billet. I'm very sorry, but an urgent matter has called me away suddenly. I don't know when I'll be back so I thought I better take everything. I didn't want to wake you up. Thank you. Goodbye. Sally.

MILLY *starts to go back upstairs.*

30. Interior. Living room. Morning. WALTER *is asleep on the put-u-up.*

ANNIE. Wally. Wake up.

He sits up.

She's gone away.

WALTER. Who?

ANNIE. She left a note. Look.

Pause while he reads.

WALTER. Yes, well . . . she . . . obviously had to go away.

Pause.

ANNIE. You didn't have any arguments with her, did you, Wally?

WALTER. No.

ANNIE. You didn't see her last night after she came back from night school?

WALTER. No.

Milly enters.

MILLY. I just found this photo in her room.

ANNIE *looks down at the photograph.*

ANNIE. A-ah. Doesn't she look lovely holding that netball. Look, Wally.

She shows WALLY *the photograph.*

MILLY. I never knew she was the games mistress. She never told us.

WALTER *puts the photograph down.*

ANNIE. It looks as though she's gone for good.

Pause.

WALTER. Yes.

Pause.

That's what it looks like.

End of play.

Revue Sketches

TROUBLE IN THE WORKS

THE BLACK AND WHITE

REQUEST STOP

LAST TO GO

SPECIAL OFFER

THE BLACK AND WHITE and TROUBLE IN THE WORKS were performed in the revue *One to Another*, which opened at the Lyric, Hammersmith on 15 July 1959.

LAST TO GO, REQUEST STOP and SPECIAL OFFER were performed in the revue *Pieces of Eight*, which opened at the Apollo Theatre, London on 23 September 1959.

TROUBLE IN THE WORKS

An office in a factory. MR. FIBBS *at the desk. A knock at the door. Enter* MR. WILLS.

FIBBS: Ah, Wills. Good. Come in. Sit down, will you?

WILLS: Thanks, Mr. Fibbs.

FIBBS: You got my message?

WILLS: I just got it.

FIBBS: Good. Good.

Pause.

Good. Well now . . . Have a cigar?

WILLS: No, thanks, not for me, Mr. Fibbs.

FIBBS: Well, now, Wills, I hear there's been a little trouble in the factory.

WILLS: Yes, I . . . I suppose you could call it that, Mr. Fibbs.

FIBBS: Well, what in heaven's name is it all about?

WILLS: Well, I don't exactly know how to put it, Mr. Fibbs.

FIBBS: Now come on, Wills, I've got to know what it is, before I can do anything about it.

WILLS: Well, Mr. Fibbs, it's simply a matter that the men have . . . well, they seem to have taken a turn against some of the products.

FIBBS: Taken a turn?

WILLS: They just don't seem to like them much any more.

FIBBS: Don't like them? But we've got the reputation of having the finest machine part turnover in the country. They're the best paid men in the industry. We've got the cheapest canteen in Yorkshire. No two menus are alike. We've got a billiard hall, haven't we, on the premises, we've got a swimming pool for use of staff. And what about the long-playing record room? And you tell me they're dissatisfied?

WILLS: Oh, the men are very grateful for all the amenities, sir. They just don't like the products.

FIBBS: But they're beautiful products. I've been in the business a lifetime. I've never seen such beautiful products.

WILLS: There it is, sir.

FIBBS: Which ones don't they like?

WILLS: Well, there's the brass pet cock, for instance.

FIBBS: The brass pet cock? What's the matter with the brass pet cock?

WILLS: They just don't seem to like it any more.

FIBBS: But what exactly don't they like about it?

WILLS: Perhaps it's just the look of it.

FIBBS: That brass pet cock? But I tell you it's perfection. Nothing short of perfection.

WILLS: They've just gone right off it.

FIBBS: Well, I'm flabbergasted.

WILLS: It's not only the brass pet cock, Mr. Fibbs.

FIBBS: What else?

WILLS: There's the hemi unibal spherical rod end.

FIBBS: The hemi unibal spherical rod end? Where could you find a finer rod end?

WILLS: There are rod ends and rod ends, Mr. Fibbs.

FIBBS: I know there are rod ends and rod ends. But where could you find a finer hemi unibal spherical rod end?

WILLS: They just don't want to have anything more to do with it.

FIBBS: This is shattering. Shattering. What else? Come on, Wills. There's no point in hiding anything from me.

WILLS: Well, I hate to say it, but they've gone very vicious about the high speed taper shank spiral flute reamers.

FIBBS: The high speed taper shank spiral flute reamers! But that's absolutely ridiculous! What could they possibly have against the high speed taper shank spiral flute reamers?

WILLS: All I can say is they're in a state of very bad agitation about them. And then there's the gunmetal side outlet relief with handwheel.

FIBBS: What!

WILLS: There's the nippled connector and the nippled adaptor and the vertical mechanical comparator.

FIBBS: No!

WILLS: And the one they can't speak about without trembling is the jaw for Jacob's chuck for use on portable drill.

FIBBS: My own Jacob's chuck? Not my very own Jacob's chuck?

WILLS: They've just taken a turn against the whole lot of them, I tell you. Male elbow adaptors, tubing nuts, grub screws, internal fan washers, dog points, half dog points, white metal bushes—

FIBBS: But not, surely not, my lovely parallel male stud couplings.

WILLS: They hate and detest your lovely parallel male stud couplings, and the straight flange pump connectors, and back nuts, and front nuts, *and* the bronzedraw off cock with handwheel and the bronzedraw off cock without handwheel!

FIBBS: Not the bronzedraw off cock with handwheel?

WILLS: And without handwheel.

FIBBS: Without handwheel?

WILLS: And with handwheel.

FIBBS: Not with handwheel?

WILLS: And without handwheel.

FIBBS: Without handwheel?

WILLS: With handwheel *and* without handwheel.

FIBBS: With handwheel *and* without handwheel?

WILLS: With or without!

Pause.

FIBBS [*broken*]: Tell me. What do they want to make in its place?

WILLS: Brandy balls.

THE BLACK AND WHITE

The FIRST OLD WOMAN *is sitting at a milk bar table. Small.*

A SECOND OLD WOMAN *approaches. Tall. She is carrying two bowls of soup, which are covered by two plates, on each of which is a slice of bread. She puts the bowls down on the table carefully.*

SECOND: You see that one come up and speak to me at the counter?

She takes the bread plates off the bowls, takes two spoons from her pocket, and places the bowls, plates and spoons.

FIRST: You got the bread, then?

SECOND: I didn't know how I was going to carry it. In the end I put the plates on top of the soup.

FIRST: I like a bit of bread with my soup.

They begin the soup. Pause.

SECOND: Did you see that one come up and speak to me at the counter?

FIRST: Who?

SECOND: Comes up to me, he says, hullo, he says, what's the time by your clock? Bloody liberty. I was just standing there getting your soup.

FIRST: It's tomato soup.

SECOND: What's the time by your clock? he says.

FIRST: I bet you answered him back.

SECOND: I told him all right. Go on, I said, why don't you get back into your scraghole, I said, clear off out of it before I call a copper.

Pause.

FIRST: I not long got here.

SECOND: Did you get the all-night bus?

FIRST: I got the all-night bus straight here.

SECOND: Where from?

FIRST: Marble Arch.

SECOND: Which one?

FIRST: The two-nine-four, that takes me all the way to Fleet
Street.

SECOND: So does the two-nine-one. [*Pause.*] I see you talking
to two strangers as I come in. You want to stop talking
to strangers, old piece of boot like you, you mind who you
talk to.

FIRST: I wasn't talking to any strangers.

Pause. The FIRST OLD WOMAN *follows the progress of a bus
through the window.*

That's another all-night bus gone down. [*Pause.*] Going
up the other way. Fulham way. [*Pause.*] That was a two-
nine-seven. [*Pause.*] I've never been up that way. [*Pause.*]
I've been down to Liverpool Street.

SECOND: That's up the other way.

FIRST: I don't fancy going down there, down Fulham way,
and all up there.

SECOND: Uh-uh.

FIRST: I've never fancied that direction much.

Pause.

SECOND: How's your bread?

Pause.

FIRST: Eh?

SECOND: Your bread.

FIRST: All right. How's yours?

Pause.

SECOND: They don't charge for the bread if you have soup.

FIRST: They do if you have tea.

SECOND: If you have tea they do. [*Pause.*] You talk to strangers they'll take you in. Mind my word. Coppers'll take you in.

FIRST: I don't talk to strangers.

SECOND: They took me away in the wagon once.

FIRST: They didn't keep you though.

SECOND: They didn't keep me, but that was only because they took a fancy to me. They took a fancy to me when they got me in the wagon.

FIRST: Do you think they'd take a fancy to me?

SECOND: I wouldn't back on it.

The FIRST OLD WOMAN *gazes out of the window.*

FIRST: You can see what goes on from this top table. [*Pause.*] It's better than going down to that place on the embankment, anyway.

SECOND: Yes, there's not too much noise.

FIRST: There's always a bit of noise.

SECOND: Yes, there's always a bit of life.

Pause.

FIRST: They'll be closing down soon to give it a scrub-round.

SECOND: There's a wind out.

Pause.

FIRST: I wouldn't mind staying.

SECOND: They won't let you.

FIRST: I know. [*Pause.*] Still, they only close hour and half, don't they? [*Pause.*] It's not long. [*Pause.*] You can go along, then come back.

SECOND: I'm going. I'm not coming back.

FIRST: When it's light I come back. Have my tea.

SECOND: I'm going. I'm going up to the Garden.

FIRST: I'm not going down there. [*Pause.*] I'm going up to Waterloo Bridge.

SECOND: You'll just about see the last two-nine-six come up over the river.

FIRST: I'll just catch a look of it. Time I get up there.

Pause.

It don't look like an all-night bus in daylight, do it?

REQUEST STOP

A queue at a Request Bus Stop. A WOMAN *at the head, with a* SMALL MAN *in a raincoat next to her, two other* WOMEN *and a* MAN.

WOMAN [*to* SMALL MAN]: I beg your pardon, what did you say?

Pause.

All I asked you was if I could get a bus from here to Shepherds Bush.

Pause.

Nobody asked you to start making insinuations.

Pause.

Who do you think you are?

Pause.

Huh. I know your sort, I know your type. Don't worry, I know all about people like you.

Pause.

We can all tell where you come from. They're putting your sort inside every day of the week.

Pause.

All I've got to do, is report you, and you'd be standing in the dock in next to no time. One of my best friends is a plain clothes detective.

Pause.

I know all about it. Standing there as if butter wouldn't melt in your mouth. Meet you in a dark alley it'd be . . . another story. [*To the others, who stare into space.*] You heard what this man said to me. All I asked him was if I could get a bus from here to Shepherds Bush. [*To him.*] I've got witnesses, don't you worry about that.

Pause.

Impertinence.

Pause.

Ask a man a civil question he treats you like a threepenny bit. [*To him.*] I've got better things to do, my lad, I can assure you. I'm not going to stand here and be insulted on a public highway. Anyone can tell you're a foreigner. I was born just around the corner. Anyone can tell you're just up from the country for a bit of a lark. I know your sort.

Pause.

She goes to a LADY.

Excuse me lady. I'm thinking of taking this man up to the magistrate's court, you heard him make that crack, would you like to be a witness?

The LADY *steps into the road.*

LADY: Taxi . . .

She disappears.

WOMAN: We know what sort she is. [*Back to position.*] I was
the first in this queue.

Pause.

Born just round the corner. Born and bred. These people
from the country haven't the faintest idea of how to behave.
Peruvians. You're bloody lucky I don't put you on a charge.
You ask a straightforward question—

*The others suddenly thrust out their arms at a passing bus.
They run off left after it. The* WOMAN, *alone, clicks her teeth
and mutters. A man walks from the right to the stop, and
waits. She looks at him out of the corner of her eye. At
length she speaks shyly, hesitantly, with a slight smile.*

Excuse me. Do you know if I can get a bus from here . . .
to Marble Arch?

LAST TO GO

A coffee stall. A BARMAN *and an old* NEWSPAPER SELLER. *The*
BARMAN *leans on his counter, the* OLD MAN *stands with tea.*
Silence.

MAN: You was a bit busier earlier.
BARMAN: Ah.
MAN: Round about ten.
BARMAN: Ten, was it?
MAN: About then.

Pause.

I passed by here about then.
BARMAN: Oh yes?
MAN: I noticed you were doing a bit of trade.

Pause.

BARMAN: Yes, trade was very brisk here about ten.
MAN: Yes, I noticed.

Pause.

I sold my last one about then. Yes. About nine forty-five.
BARMAN: Sold your last then, did you?
MAN: Yes, my last 'Evening News' it was. Went about twenty
to ten.

Pause.

BARMAN: 'Evening News', was it?
MAN: Yes.

Pause.

Sometimes it's the 'Star' is the last to go.
BARMAN: Ah.
MAN: Or the . . . whatsisname.
BARMAN: 'Standard'.
MAN: Yes.

Pause.

All I had left tonight was the 'Evening News'.

Pause.

BARMAN: Then that went, did it?
MAN: Yes.

Pause.

Like a shot.

Pause.

BARMAN: You didn't have any left, eh?

MAN: No. Not after I sold that one.

Pause.

BARMAN: It was after that you must have come by here then, was it?

MAN: Yes, I come by here after that, see, after I packed up.

BARMAN: You didn't stop here though, did you?

MAN: When?

BARMAN: I mean, you didn't stop here and have a cup of tea then, did you?

MAN: What, about ten?

BARMAN: Yes.

MAN: No, I went up to Victoria.

BARMAN: No, I thought I didn't see you.

MAN: I had to go up to Victoria.

Pause.

BARMAN: Yes, trade was very brisk here about then.

Pause.

MAN: I went to see if I could get hold of George.

BARMAN: Who?

MAN: George.

Pause.

BARMAN: George who?

MAN: George . . . whatsisname.

BARMAN: Oh.

Pause.

Did you get hold of him?

MAN: No. No, I couldn't get hold of him. I couldn't locate him.

BARMAN: He's not about much now, is he?

Pause.

MAN: When did you last see him then?

BARMAN: Oh, I haven't seen him for years.

MAN: No, nor me.

Pause.

BARMAN: Used to suffer very bad from arthritis.
MAN: Arthritis?
BARMAN: Yes.
MAN: He never suffered from arthritis.
BARMAN: Suffered very bad.

Pause.

MAN: Not when I knew him.

Pause.

BARMAN: I think he must have left the area.

Pause.

MAN: Yes, it was the 'Evening News' was the last to go tonight.
BARMAN: Not always the last though, is it, though?
MAN: No. Oh no. I mean sometimes it's the 'News'. Other times it's one of the others. No way of telling beforehand. Until you've got your last one left, of course. Then you can tell which one it's going to be.
BARMAN: Yes.

Pause.

MAN: Oh yes.

Pause.

I think he must have left the area.

SPECIAL OFFER

SECRETARY (*at a desk in an office*): Yes, I was in the rest room at Swan and Edgars, having a little rest. Just sitting there, interfering with nobody, when this old crone suddenly came right up to me and sat beside me. You're on the staff of the B.B.C. she said, aren't you? I've got just the thing for you, she said, and put a little card into my hand. Do you know what was written on it? MEN FOR SALE! What on earth do you mean? I said. Men, she said, all sorts shapes and sizes, for sale. What on earth can you *possibly mean*? I said. It's an international congress, she said, got up for the entertainment and relief of lady members of the civil service. You can hear some of the boys we've got speak through a microphone, especially for your pleasure, singing little folk tunes we're sure you've never heard before. Tea is on the house and every day we have the very best pastries. For the cabaret at teatime the boys do a rare dance imported all the way from Buenos Aires, dressed in nothing but a pair of cricket pads. Every single one one of them is tried and tested, very best quality, and at very reasonable rates. If you like one of them by any of his individual characteristics you can buy him, but for you not at retail price. As you work for the B.B.C. we'll be glad to make a special reduction. If you're at all dissatisfied you can send him back within seven days and have your money refunded. That's *very* kind of you, I said, but as a matter of fact I've just been on leave, I start work tomorrow and am perfectly refreshed. And I left her where she was. Men for Sale! What an extraordinary idea! I've never heard of anything so outrageous, have you? Look – here's the card.

Pause.

Do you think it's a joke . . . or serious?